'The Invasion ... vention in ou... continuing re... anticipation.' ... *Supplement*

'The Invasion Handbook is a disturbing, fascinating book, the first of a trilogy, which I shall certainly keep on my shelves somewhere between the poetry section and the horrifying volumes of 20th-ce... Primo Levi, the Klemperer diaries, t... Arendt to Heidegger.' A. N. Wilson,

'Erudite, playful, obscure, dramatic a... *The Invasion Handbook* presents a c... perspectives, from that of Lenin to that of Churchill, from Walter Benjamin to Trotsky, Bakunin to Speer.' Helen Meany, *Irish Times*

'Tom Paulin is among the best of a great generation of Irish poets.' *Sunday Telegraph*

'Tom Paulin writes an extraordinary language, even when he's not inventing words or exhibiting some unsuspected prize from the hoard of Irish English.' *Guardian*

Tom Paulin was born in Leeds in 1949 grew up in Belfast, and was educated at the universities of Hull and Oxford. He has published six other volumes of poetry as well as a *Selected Poems 1972–1990*, two major anthologies, versions of Greek drama, and several critical works. Well known for his appearances on the BBC's *Late Review*, he is also the G. M. Young Lecturer in English at Hertford College, Oxford.

TOM PAULIN

The Invasion Handbook

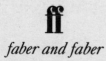

faber and faber

First published in 2002
by Faber and Faber Limited
3 Queen Square London WC1N 3AU
Published in the United States by Faber and Faber Inc.
an affiliate of Farrar, Straus and Giroux LLC, New York
This paperback edition first published in 2003

Photoset by Wilmaset Ltd, Birkenhead, Wirral
Printed in England by Bookmarque Ltd, Croydon

A CIP record for this book
is available from the British Library

ISBN 0–571–21858–X

ACKNOWLEDGEMENTS
*BBC Radio Three, The Dublin Review, London Review of Books,
Modern Painters, The Observer, Poetry Review, Times Literary
Supplement.*

I am grateful to the National Endowment for Science,
Technology and the Arts for a fellowship. – T.P.

10 9 8 7 6 5 4 3 2 1

Contents

The Invasion Handbook

Prologue

Koba is in a country
no a wilderness province
the size of Scotland
– nine months of ice and snow
they live in caves where his fellow
exiles fear the hard glints
in his eyes his yellow
smoky eyes that hex his comrades
and will them toward the shades
summer's hot – they move to shacks and tents
– the tents sailcloth the shacks tarred
always aloof and solitary
he imagines becoming the metal Shah
the steel Tsar I mean
of all the Russias
gravedigger hangman knotting his rope
the hardest of hard cases
he will one day forge – yes *forge*
a new a rigid Europe
but for this stretch he's on the far mar-
gins of a wrinkled no not a withered state
that's broken at the head and hips
alone on the taiga
– a clanging bird somewhere –
he places a juniper berry on his lips
sucks then rolls it on his tongue
a tiny bit of gunge
it tastes quite deliciously bitter
now with one
one as yet undreaded hand
he scratches his head for a long long

time like a patient tiger
though in his best and worst dreams
this drunken shoemaker's son
is Caesar inside a nutmeg or an almond
the king of infinite space
with the power to bring the world to an end
though all these four long years
he knows he has pitched his tent
upon a grain of sand

Clemenceau

'faut commencer avec Clemenceau
in no way clement
and forbidding like a pot palm
– sterile and fruitless
his pitted cheeks scurfbark
in a room dry like a hotpress
where they tried le Conseil des Quatres
to live the dead
to grind peace into its opposite
as though they'd met in a stranded diningcar
inside the Hall of Mirrors
to sing a psalm –
when Israel went into Egypt
there was heard the plockplock of horsehooves
a toltering bustle clipped scatter
like sabots clocking the cobbles
in some Rhineland town
black as the cavern null and void
of the Empire fireplace
in that hot dry room
with its marble its leafy mirror
the glass dome over a snowy owl
un hibou blanc comme une colombe
brooding on a black abyss
or as snow falling softly
so very very softly
like leaves millions of leaves
reeling down on all those
who would say if they could
I am not yet born
while out of the night and the snow

rises the hunting sovereign dove
as these four men the cloud compellers
weigh Germany's guilt like gold or diamonds
or a tiny heap of dust
in the shivering trivial
skittery unforgiving balance

no one knows that I Georges Clemenceau
– I the Tiger
no one knows I made war
with 40 grammes of sugar in my blood
senem annis animo juvenum
– the Latin orator in the Sheldonian
made me Christ the Tiger
in the juvescence – wrong springy word –
of the year
the cruel time of the year
my father a Jacobin
who hung a portrait of Robespierre
a portrait of St Just
in our house in the Vendée
– marsh plain bocage
I have been faithful to our good earth
to Dreyfus
and have been ever and always an enemy
to the guillotine
though Rodin's bust it makes me
a Mongolian general
my apartment is brimful
of Manets and Monets
– long before I wrote
my book – heart of light – on *Les Nymphéas*
Monet gave me *Le Bloc*

the prophet's mountain top
for it was given this prophet to more than know
that the Germans are a peuple servile
that needs force
to support an argument
– Napoleon before he died
said that nothing fixed
nothing permanent
can be founded on force
me I'm not so sure
a hundred years for you Americans
is a very long time
for us it's not much
I've known men who saw Napoleon
with their own eyes
America is faraway
protected by the Ocean
England couldn't be reached
by Napoleon himself
you are both of you safe
we are not

The Skeleton

(after Verlaine)

Two pachles both stocious are lurching back
over a battlefield – they're doubles of our old friend
the miles gloriosus and they look bulky like sacks
so maybe they're Hessians who like Jack Falstaff
are – mortal men sir – full of sack
and sorry the war has staggered to an end
but then they see this gnawed daft
– nit of a translator says *deboned* – skeleton
lying there among the puddles and shellholes
the mud the debris the bust or abandoned weapons
– like a trapdoor its mouth gapes open
as it lies there static a bleached symbol of ending
then Captain Bones cranks up and addresses our two
    squaddies
– more to come – tell the ranks – more great more
    dulce days!

The Four

Toi au Premier Instant
tu étais présent
avec tes puissantes ailes éployées

comme une colombe
tu couras l'immense Abîme
et tu le rendais fécond

You have not forgotten me. Some of you even remember my parents in the Abbey, at my funeral service. But you have forgotten these words, though you know the poem an American, another American in Europe, like Woodrow Wilson, made of them. You extract a banal, consoling message from his epic fragment – rootlessness, modern civilization too secular – I haven't time to spell out its tedium. The tedium of the message, not the poem.

Paris was a nightmare and everyone there was morbid. Levity, blindness, insolence – confused cries from without – all the elements of ancient tragedy were there. An occasional visit to the hot dry room in the President's house, where the Four fulfilled their destinies in empty and arid intrigue, only added to the sense of nightmare. The figure and bearing of Clemenceau are universally familiar. At the Council of Four he wore a square-tailed coat of very good, thick and black broadcloth, and on his hands, which were

---

The Treaty of Versailles, 28 June 1919, made peace between the Allies and Germany. Under this Carthaginian Peace, Germany lost territory and its colonies, and had limitations placed on its armed forces. Heavy reparations were also imposed, the Rhineland was demilitarized and occupied, and the union of Germany and Austria was forbidden. The Germans signed the Treaty under protest (there was a notorious 'war-guilt clause'), but a large section of public opinion in France and Britain felt that its terms were not sufficiently harsh.

never uncovered, grey suede – no, silk – gloves. His boots were of thick black leather, very good, but with a country style, and sometimes fastened in front, curiously, by a buckle instead of laces. His seat was on a square brocaded chair. He sat on that square brocaded chair in the middle of a semi-circle facing the fireplace. Signor Orlando on his left, with President Wilson, then the Prime Minister, Lloyd George, on the other side. He held no papers and no portfolio. Conserving his strength, he spoke seldom. He closed his eyes often, impassive, a face of parchment. His sudden outbursts of words were followed by deep coughing.

Throned on the brocaded chair, in his grey silk gloves, dry in soul and empty of hope, Clemenceau was very old and tired, but he surveyed the scene with a cynical and almost impish air. And when at last silence was restored, it was to discover that he had disappeared.

He felt about France what Pericles felt about Athens – a unique value in her, nothing else mattering; but his theory of politics was Bismarck's. His was the policy of an old man, whose most vivid impressions and most lively imagination are of the past and not of the future. Once, listening to Wilson, he became so angry, he snapped an ivory paperknife.

Wilson's head and features are finely cut and exactly like his photograph. Like Odysseus he looked wiser when he was seated. His hands, though capable and strong, are wanting in sensitiveness and finesse. His egoism, isolation, icy ignorance and mulishness are classically presbyterian, the Scotch Irish variety. A theological cast of mind, not intellectual. He is neither a student nor a scholar, nor is he exquisitely cultivated like Clemenceau or Balfour. Like a blind and deaf Don Quixote, he was insensitive to his surroundings. He was not sensitive to his audience or environment at all, and had no chance against Lloyd George's unerring, almost medium-like sensibility to everyone immediately around him. He had no plan, no scheme, no constructive ideas. Slow and unadaptable and ill-informed, he was caught up in the toils of the Old World.

We will get out of Germany all you can squeeze out of a lemon and a bit more. I will squeeze her until you can hear the pips squeak.

Unlike the fool Geddes I can hear the pips scream. Lamp faces with puckering mouths. We are without the experience of the psychology of a white race under conditions little short of servitude. German democracy is thus annihilated at the very moment when the German people was about to build it up after a severe struggle – annihilated by the very persons who throughout the war never tired of maintaining that they sought to bring democracy to us. Germany is no longer a people and a state, but becomes a mere trade concern placed by its creditors in the hands of a receiver.

The policy of reducing Germany to servitude for a generation, of degrading the lives of millions of human beings, and of depriving a whole nation of happiness should be abhorrent and detestable – as abhorrent and detestable even if it were possible, even if it enriched ourselves, even if we did not sow the decay of the whole civilized life of Europe. Some preach it in the name of Justice. In the great events of man's history, in the unwinding of the complex fates of nations, Justice is not so simple. And if it were, nations are not authorized, by religion or by natural morals, to visit on the children of their enemies the misdoings of parents or of rulers. I tell you, this is a Carthaginian Peace. We are sowing the earth with salt – I can see divisions of Freikorps rising out of it, dozens upon dozens, like leathery eggs.

The fundamental economic problem of a Europe starving and disintegrating before their eyes was the one question in which it was impossible to arouse the interest of the Four. The sameness was also striking. One devastated area was exactly like another – a heap of rubble, a morass of shell holes and straggle of wire. Each like a massproduced exhibit in a roofless gallery, and then as the guilt from that detached insult – that comparison – began to bite, each was nothing and nowhere, which was worse, because more empty and detached.

Those who sign this Treaty will sign the death sentence of many millions of German men, women and children. I look at the exhaustion of the soil, the breakdown of the European railway system, the breakdown of the European currency system. As Lenin remarked, the best way to destroy the capitalist system is to debauch the currency. The forces of the nineteenth century have run their course and are exhausted. As I write, the flames of Russian Bolshevism seem, for the moment at least, to have burnt themselves out, and the peoples of Central and Eastern Europe are held in a dreadful torpor. The lately gathered harvest keeps off the worst privations, and Peace has been declared at Paris. But winter approaches.

If we aim deliberately at the impoverishment of Central Europe, vengeance, I dare predict, will not limp. Nothing can then delay for very long that final civil war between the forces of Reaction and the despairing convulsions of Revolution, before which the horrors of the late German war will fade into nothing, and which will destroy, whoever is victor, the civilization and progress of our generation. I foresee a new military power establishing itself in the East, with its spiritual home in Brandenburg, drawing to itself all military talent and all the military adventurers, all those who regret emperors and hate democracy, in the whole of eastern and central and south-eastern Europe. A power which would be geographically inaccessible to the military forces of the Allies might well be found, at least in the anticipations of the timid – a new Napoleonic domination, rising, as by a phoenix, from the ashes of cosmopolitan militarism.

In this autumn of 1919, in which I write, we are at the dead season of our fortunes. The reaction from the exertions, the fears, and the sufferings of the past five years is at its height. After such knowledge, we neither know nor practise forgiveness.

5/6/19
Dear Prime Minister,
I ought to let you know that on Saturday I am slipping away from the scene of the nightmare. I can do no more good here. I've gone on hoping even through these last dreadful weeks that you'd find some way to make the Treaty a just and expedient document. But now it's apparently too late. The battle is lost. I leave the Twins to gloat over the devastation of Europe, and to assess to taste what remains for the British taxpayer.

Sincerely yours,
J. M. Keynes

Mantoux

I Etienne Mantoux
– killed in action near the Danube
a few days before our victory
I dare from the brink
of this bright sinister river
– this playground river
as it was and will be
I dare in my turn to predict
that nothing can delay for very long
that enormous that super
state or bank we came so close to
when Hitler's armies
washed their tank tracks
in La Manche – it is a fact
that though he was wrong very wrong
the Appeasers those who cried mea culpa
and failed to enforce the Treaty
they had Baron Keynes to thank
for throwing us all together
like rats in a sack

The Former Yugoslavia

It may seem crazy
but first the Serbs
defeated us – us Habsburgs –
and then they badly beat us
when we were Nazis
so we waited in the dark
waited till the last century's
skin was nearly shed
and Tito's concrete ark
would and could not float
then we – that is us Austrians
(keep it soggy)
Germans and Italians
took a deep stale breath
that stank of ancient puss
– puss and piss
the double dead –
then we told Slovenia
and Croatia
go you your own ways
make sure you wreck
Versailles and this late
late new Europe
– study how to hate
for no matter how many deaths
they'll tie themselves
in knots the Serbs –
and though it's our rope
the free world'll punish and blame
– no not Trudj-
man and the others –

but only those stiffnecked
those headbanging Serbs
– it's from our pobby grudges
at their victories
these new massacres stem

Techne

Orts and scraps torn stamps bits of debris
staled by other men and women
more random than the nicks on a tallystick
or like Lepidus
meet only to be sent on errands
so not freestanding not sovereign
once they're taken
– taken and used

now I plunge my hand again
into a wallet that's greasy
and without the frame
– no the idea –
of form or shape
though like a pilgrim
what we call time
or call anxiety and fear
has that slimy wallet on its back
and as I feel inside this slippery
this drecky sack
like someone fingering a spittoon for alms
I try to hear a snatch of music
that stands solemn
– though it's not a psalm –
solemn but a bit sticky
like a lip or prittstick
– *but where's the carol the creation?*
ah answering that question
it makes me anxious
this music though can take licks

the way a stamp does
or some hero in a paper
I mean a looseleaf epic

Imago 1919

The sense of uncanniness
                    Jentsch identifies the essential
                    factor
in this feeling's production
                    as intellectual uncertainty
so that the uncanny
                    would as it were
                    be always
something one does not know one's way about in
heimlich is thus a word
                    the meaning of which
                    develops
in the direction of ambivalence
                    develops until it finally
                    coincides with its opposite
                    unheimlich
I recall that on certain evenings
                    his mother
                    my patient's mother
used to send the children to bed early
                    the Sand Man is coming
                    she told them
the Sand Man whose hands
                    were sifting claws
he was going to pull out their eyes
                    and eat them
one hot summer afternoon
                    it happened I was walking
through the empty streets
of a provincial town in Italy
                    a bleared shabby town

                                             that was unknown to me
I found myself in a quarter
                                 of whose character
                                 like the smell of cat stale
I could not long remain in doubt
        nothing but women
                 painted women
were to be seen at the windows
                                 of the small houses
and I made haste to leave the narrow street
                                 at the next turning
but after having wandered about
                                 for a time
without inquiring my way
                                 I found myself suddenly back
                                 in the same narrow street
where now my presence was beginning
        to excite attention
                                 I hurried once more away
only to arrive by another détour
at the same place yet a third time
        now however a feeling overcame me
a feeling I can only describe
                                 as uncanny
and I was glad enough
                                 to find myself back
                                 at the piazza
it had a bronze
                                 perhaps baroque fountain
the piazza I had left
                                 a short while before
without any further voyages of discovery
                                 let me say this

                            one of the most uncanny
                            most widespread forms
of superstition is the dread
                                   of the evil eye
                            a superstition
that has been studied exhaustively
     by the Hamburg oculist
     Seligmann
                            if we take the German
                            expression the phrase
     in an unheimlich house
we find that some languages in use today
     can only render an unheimlich house
     as a haunted house
now you may want to inquire
                       why did I not conceal
that is paint over
     my return to that quarter
                            of the painted ladies?
for it is almost clear
     that on one level
                            I wished to return there
even in the first instance to go there
                            and that my détour
was in fact to the piazza
     where I abandoned
                            my voyages of discovery
in your language I quite well know
what it is the verbs to cover and to paint
     mean
because in the end I wish to be read
          as you read Shakespeare
          or those copies of Strand Magazine

that in the middle
of the isolation of wartime
fell into my hands
and among other
somewhat redundant matter
I read a story about a young couple
recently married
who move into a furnished house
in which there is a
curiously shaped table
possibly of teak
on which are carvings
carvings of crocodiles
towards evening an intolerable
and very specific smell
the fishy odour of the old Nile serpent
begins to pervade the house
they stumble over
something in the dark
as a story it was naive enough
but the feeling it produced
was quite remarkable
I confess I saw Rome
melt into the Tiber
concerning the factors of silence
silence and darkness
we can only assert
that they
are actually elements
in the causes of infantile anxiety
from which most people
have never become free

Bracken at Sedbergh

Poor dear Brendan
is opening his cheque book
in the headmaster's study
– no this is the dreamtime
bright beaming young Brendan
is nineteen
going on fifteen
and he holds his pen
like a glossy hazel wand
– holds it in his right hand
that's near as big as Tasmania
his skin it's papery
like a eucalyptus leaf
his back straight
as a beech tree
skin hard like oak bark
and his eyes bright as the blossom
on a boortree
he has travelled indeed
a long way from Tipperary
and Weech can see he isn't dumb
– big bold Brendan
opens his cheque book
a book not as ornate maybe
as our intricate Book of Kells
indeed it might be more fit
for a character on the far edge
of a Wilde play
the top cheque looks sunbleached
for it has travelled with jolly swagmen
(friends mayhap of the late Ned Kelly)

through the deserts of Australia
where all men each
and every one are mates are equal
but Brendan like that hero Magwitch
or a ticket of leave man
a returned Fenian
(alas they failed to seize Canada
for our sorrowing nation)
– Brendan has bobbed up from down under
like a cork – pronounced *cark* –
and he looks the boul Brendan
as if he's been dragged through a hedge
then left in the sun
or a handbag like the child Oedipus
but that ever so slight
shiver as he signs his name
must mean he's spent a cold night a darksome
night in the gripe of a ditch
howsomever the sweet tenor Brendanus
wields his pen like a loy
and digs deep into the paper
where of course – of coorse –
he strikes oil
for behold this is the moment
when our hero enters
into the kingdom of heaven
by which we mean the Commons
by which we mean the House of Lords
– in his neat sleek craft
St Brendan is rowing toward that moment which
will be absolute will be crucial
that is the moment when he'll
by the exercise of the purest skill

nudge Winston into position
and so by enormous hook
and by enormous crook
this master politician
this Alexander
will shape history
through that former naval person

With the Setting Sun

He might have scorched his hat
and brushed down a star
as one dewy dusk he felt himself falling
– a soft fall – surprising –
over the Starnbergersee
the air warm spicy
still with the noonheat in it
as he made a long languorous descent
an airman with a machinegun
and high leather boots
– officers' boots
swinging under the silk canopy
of his parachute
and dropping dropping toward this inland sea
whose loop widened into a mirror
of Europe's central sea
as below him he saw
the limber leg of Italy
Athens and the Cyclades
then on the far rim next France and Holland
the timber leg of Britain
fenced by ocean
and not for the taking – at least not yet –
his slow descent was like rising
into a victory so famous
the shades of Alexander and Napoleon
– all the great generals – would be jealous
yes this smallholder
this petit caporal would one day inherit
an estate so enormous
the world itself could not contain it

Weimar

Ernst Jünger, he sees a whole new race smart strong and filled with will.

One day in 1919 the Republic no one wanted was born.

The Republic with a hole in its heart.

On 9 November 1918, Friedrich Ebert became Chancellor for one day. Then in February the following year he was elected President, though at the installation ceremony the oath was found to be missing. So an ex-tailor proclaimed an ex-saddler the new leader of Germany. The Weimar Republic, it was said, should avoid ceremonies as a governess should avoid dancing ballet.

When the machineguns opened up, the crowd fled, but it avoided crossing the ex-Kaiser's lawn.

Berlin – a Babylonian bottomless deep – at once chaotic and compelling.

Toller's regime lasted six days – under it a new economic concept – Schwundgeld – vanishing money – was invented. It was decreed that each week the mark would lose 1/1000th value.

Du matin
jusqu'au midi
il roula
du midi
jusqu'au soir
d'un jour d'été
et avec le soleil
couchant
il s'abattit
du zénith
comme une étoile
tombante

When Dr Lipp became People's Commissar for Foreign Affairs, he proclaimed *The proletariat of Upper Bavaria is united. Socialists and independent socialists and communists are firmly as one, together with the farmers' union. The liberal bourgeoisie has been totally exposed as Prussian agents. Cowardly former comrade Hoffmann who fled taking with him the keys to the lavatory is now established at Bamberg and receiving food and coal in tremendous quantities from Switzerland and Italy. We want peace for ever, Immanuel Kant, Von Ewiger Freiheit, 1795. Prussia only wants an armistice to prepare for her revenge.*

Lipp filled the Foreign Office with red carnations.

Lipp was concerned at a puddle that was found in the ex-king's bathroom, because the king might have spent hours playing with toy boats.

When Lipp was asked to resign, he said 'Even this will I do for the Republic.'

As was customary, Munich sweeps had little red flags on their carts. When the Freikorps shot at them, the sweeps explained that they were not communists.

Communists were gutshot by firing-squads.

A bullet hit Rubes – no not Rubens – in the Zwinger Gallery. Kokoschka appealed not to indulge in warlike activities in front of the gallery.

In the train back to Berlin after the fall of Kapp, most members of the government got drunk and vomited in each other's compartments.

Once again he was the fantasist and drop-out, the rejected and unrecognized artistic genius in the dingy room in the Stumpergasse, who had found his idol in the master of Bayreuth.

All the wheels are standing still
when it is the workers' will

The occupation of the Rhineland led to galloping inflation.

1923 was the year of the great inflation.

Disgusted by its worthlessness, a beggar threw a 100,000 mark note in the gutter.

There was an obsession with food, an almost sexual relation to food.

Traditional middle-class morality disappeared overnight.

Cross-dressing became very popular.

Inflation came under control when the Roggenmark, the rye mark, was introduced.

Hitler was seen as a comic figure. Auer, the SPD leader, disagreed and wanted to deport him.

In 1921, the Bavarian interior minister proposed to deport Hitler.

Hitler at high society banquets didn't know how to eat artichoke. He would spoon sugar into vintage wines.

Hitler was put under fortress arrest. This was a punishment traditionally reserved for 'naughty boys' of good family who'd killed their man in a duel.

Hitler in Bavarian costume (rejected) 1925/6.
Hitler with his alsatian, Prinz, 1925 (rejected, from a broken plate).
Hitler in a raincoat (accepted), 1925/6.

Cigars made of cabbage leaves.

In public lavatories, notices stated *No later than two hours after having sexual intercourse proceed to nearest clinic.*

Ersatz coffee in the Café Josty where each metal coffee pot had a little glove on the handle to prevent fingers being burnt.

Berliners are schlagfertig – ready to strike, always with a reply on the tip of the tongue. They never returned a Nazi majority.

Berlin became a world city – a Weltstadt – in the 20s.

The void that had been filled by monarchy and aristocrats was now filled mostly by a crowd of intellectuals, journalists and film stars.

Everything on the sexual front was permitted.

Domel pretended to be Prince William of Prussia and moved from one first-class hotel to another.

Pieter Kurten, the Düsseldorf mass murderer.

Karl Denke sold human flesh smoked in jars as goat's meat.

Republican politics had a colourless quality that was German thoroughness in a grey anonymous state free of glamour or a leading principle which could provide a rallying point.

Rathenau, the foreign minister, was killed because he was an excellent minister and a Jew.

The usual fate of leftwing extremists – shot while trying to escape.

Hitler in private said that Stresemann was the greatest German politician since Bismarck.

In magazines aimed at white collar workers there are advertisements for pens, Kohinoor pencils, haemorrhoid treatments, hair loss, beds, crêpe soles, white teeth, rejuvenation treatments, coffee consumption habits, dictaphones, writer's cramp, trembling particularly in the presence of others, quality pianos on weekly instalments.

They teach Kant and live off the interest.

Mussolini arrived at the Quirinal Palace in a crumpled black shirt, white spats and bowler hat.

Of Berlin Goebbels said the spirit of the asphalt democracy is piled high.

Little by little, there was a revulsion in our favour. Now and then a policeman would come and whisper into our ears that he was at heart on our side.

Contrary as it appears to all received opinion, Hitler had a mind. It was coarse, turbid, narrow, rigid, cruel, but it was a mind. A terrible phenomenon, that mind, imposing indeed in its granitic harshness and yet infinitely squalid in its miscellaneous cumber – like some huge barbarian monolith, the expression of giant strength and savage genius, surrounded by a festering heap of refuse – old tins and dead vermin, ashes and eggshells and ordure – the intellectual detritus of centuries. (As I write this, I notice that the college cat – he is called Simkins – is crossing the quad.)

Merz

must be Schmerz
of course I twitter am
– I Schwitters am
in this – let's call it tin –
mirror to the which
I've stuck a tram ticket
for my Fahrscheinbild
whose inwit – or is it un? –
chucks a dead light
on all those journeys
ending at the Himmelfarb
– the railway lines the loaded guns
the – cheap phrase for fate –
the ultimate bad luck
then – no you can't duck it –
then wirenetting
flake of bark from a silver birch
– another fluke –
a pram wheel the label
from a jamjar its purple
undusty plum
plus string cottonwool
as I steal
unseen to west with this disgrace
and stay there stumm
as barren as a wooden perch
– it is that woodiness I try to trace
so dry so dumb
add a tin can
– that always hurts
teat cut from a condom

(note the internal rhyme)
and note all these
all these have equal value
with applied paint
in my cathedral
of erotic misery
its strong toil
– that is *net*
strong toil of grace
the sting in its tail
another piece of string
and a lost child
where what to me is Schmiere
is grease
to you's *a kind
of faecal smearing*
just pure shite
no stainedglass saint
glowing inside a church
where these bits – little bits and pieces
call them des bribes et des morceaux en
plein air – I mean plain air
are fixed with glue
and yet to say they're preserved
– well like faeces –
is to miss the way each series
of matched jerks
(here you desire Miss Susan Stirk)
– the way each series
by this maybe cabotin
asserts the necessary the found beauty
I have called Merz
which – I'll be terse – is art scraped

*To beat the Negro
efficiently
therefore requires
a cane, but it has
to be a split one,
so that the cane
will cause wounds
large enough
to prevent
suppuration
beneath the
Negro's thick skin.*
Immanuel Kant

right back from the edge
– after rubble
I'll learn for sure to say *Ribble*
and rest among the poet Lakes
maybe make another sculpture
of bread and porridge

An Indefinite Article

There was a queasiness
as the house turned quiet
it was quiet like a deserted office
on a Saturday or a Sunday
but he didn't consider its emptiness
– that neap or ebbed feeling –
when he returned as usual to his office
early the next morning and worked late
then on the way to the lavatory
he looked down into a little square courtyard
– *a* not *the* courtyard –
that was surrounded by offices
all the windows were dark
but the opposite panes on the top storey
cast back a faint reflection of the moon
he tried to make out the shapes in one corner
of the courtyard – they were wooden
handbarrows jumbled together
and they made him feel sorry
that he had been unable to prevent
the flogging in the lumber room
even so it seemed to him
that the crooked timber of humanity
was now on the straight and narrow
he lived in a fairly flat country
with a legal constitution
there was universal peace
all the laws were in force
he was a bank manager

not a housepainter
– who would dare to seize
him in his own dwelling?

Locarno One

oh so easy so facile
like light verse
or a trick cyclist
moving between two crags
where a chamois climbs
– no leaps airily airily leaps
by abrupt and intricate ways
like Burke's gothic his irregular style
as he headbutts the Aufklärung
our Enlightenment
its ever so confident rungs
and ways that go straight
as a masonic ruler through the woods
except that double *o* is the void
– quite without form
and with no brooding stockdove
no roucoulement
warming two white eggs
in what abyss
a cuas between plump stately mountains
that taper to a summit
and reflect the sun like tents
like Agamemnon's ample tent

In October 1925, an important international conference was held in
the Swiss lake resort of Locarno. The conference produced a number
of treaties which rewrote the Treaty of Versailles and brought
Germany back into the European fold and into the League of Nations.
The treaties were a triumph for the British foreign secretary, Austen
Chamberlain, the French foreign minister, Aristide Briand, and the
German foreign minister, Gustav Stresemann, who sought
international cooperation. Among the reporters at the conference was
Jerome K. Jerome, famous for his comic novel *Three Men in a Boat*.

– instead of a dove
but in search of that white irenic creature
that will fly or appear to fly
out of Austen Chamberlain's top hat
Jerome K. Jerome sits in his hotel room
– blue blazer glinty brass buttons
he knows he has two years to live
that he saw the smashed fields of Flanders
and that like a straw boater
his initial hides the name Klapka
– if Locarno is that cyclist
on a tightrope
on a tied trope
Parme is a compact
an almost cloying name
stifling as an airless
stifling as a lunk
summer's evening
here there's no performer
whose perfect balance
rests on calculation and goodwill
not on direct or applied force
as JKJ
types this thin thing happening
that might be a stele
on the road to the Treaty of Rome

why come back then
to the Princesse de Parme?
to some perfumer
impregnating a solid block of fat
with the scent of a hundred thousand violets?
– because Locarno wanted to do away

with war and harm
as though a lank-
y waiter could serve us breakfast
with neither bacon nor ham
or hand a simple slice
of unrobed melon on a plate
and say
who'd have believed
flesh ever could be sliced
so very very thin?

who'd have believed
the airy thinness
of our paper darts and gliders
riding the thermals?
not Olof Palme
who ended bashed on the pavement
like yesterday's newspaper
not that stamped bar of soap
– rendered soap
found on a shelf
in a drogheria in Bolzano
one summer's day in 68

perfectly beautiful
Locarno's a nice little town
rather Italian than Swiss in character
tucked under high mountains
on the shores of the Lake
– but why did the high contracting parties
choose Locarno or Luggarus?
why because the Germans
wanted somewhere that wasn't French
the French

somewhere that wasn't German
and Austen Chamberlain
an Alpine orchid for his buttonhole
and a resort where Mussolini could drop in
like a parachutist landing lightly
on a Palace garden party
an occasion where HRH Prince of Wales
the Parachute Regiment's colonel in chief
might just be about
to shake Gerry Adams by the hand
— *if he were an Englishman in England*
Mussolini would not be a fascist
Clemmie praised his beautiful
oh those golden brown piercing eyes
and Winston his great simple bearing
his calm detached poise
— a Caesar and a perfect man
spreading maps in a tent
chunk chin and shaved head
like a fence post
— its eyes fixed upon nothing
this gruff baste
lifts a paw to the crowd
among them a pressman
waiting to file his copy
— *fascist rule is corrupt incompetent empty*
Mussolini arrives like a loud
maître d'hôtel
who doubles as a nightclub bouncer
or a sweaty wrestler
— six bodyguards
braced on the runningboard
of his open Lancia

– they're fenceposts in suits
he's an armsdealer
out of a Shaw play
– his Lancia guns on the bend
it sweeps up the slopes of St Bernard
where the vines are cut back bare as testicles
– from here
Napoleon saw the Italian plains
spread below him like a field of light
but this is the road the track
of the unblessed
where a pocket Orion
staggers into the sunrise
like Rousseau moving toward Paris
– you see Clemmie says you see
but can't ever look at those eyes
it's such an awful pity

c'est comme une accouchement dans une gare!
Briand groans one night in the Pretorio
then sends a press release to the French people
– it's the final settlement this
while Stresemann he tells the Germans
Locarno is the freedom
to win our freedom

Locarno Two

6 December 1917

Daheim – Pension Daheim –
dat's in a sense familiar
– somewhere between Heim
and Dasein but that taints
this neat dovegrey
almost official guesthouse
that's only a stage a post
in his meandery journey
(do I mean Derry?
I'm after catching another voice
and then another)
for this – the Pension Daheim –
is where JAJ
writes to Henry Sykes
about typing his manuscript
(he hears the clatter of those *t*s on the platen
even though his pen is inking the page)
it's the feeling polpastrelli
as Mulligan's fingers
touch his jaw and chin
the trill of the afterscrape
of sharp steel on skin wet
soapy skin whose pores
are unclosed by any aftershave
– it's that touchiness concerns him
he reports the cat
and others are well
he asks Sykes to arrange the typing
with a friend of his

– Mr Rudolf Goldschmidt
a Swiss grain merchant
and he reports he's at work now
on the last part of the Telemachia
– even as he writes he's rejecting
polpastrelli – it's the palps
of Mulligan's fingers
those thick beefy feelers
that touch him now
– a hit aye
a very palpable hit
as the shivery rain outside
makes him feel at home
it's steely this rain
– come up Kinch you fearful Jesuit
don't you know there's a war on?

Just a few days after Professor Sidler
had performed an iridectomy on his right eye
JAJ a halfwounded halfblind Orion
met a young woman Dr Gertrude Kaempffer
who three weeks before'd been cured of TB
– a miracle! said the pensionnaire
delicate shy beautiful
when Gertrude held out her hand in farewell
he stroked it
– what fine slender hands you have
please will you write me
poste restante in Zürich?
I want to tell you how furiously I jiggled
when my nanny suddenly squatted on the ground
and pissed full till we heard the earth scatter
I want to make you

into Miss Gerty MacDowell
whose eyes will be
of the bluest Irish blue
set off by lustrous lashes and dark expressive brows
and I want to take your name
– to take Kaempffer
and every so often lick it
touch it with my tongue
– they would both have brekky
simple but perfectly served
– there wasn't a brack on them
– the little kinnet
– some poet chap with bearsgrease plastery hair
lovelock over his dexter optic
– my arks she called it
(meaning of course her arse)
– up like a rocket
down like a stick

now he stalks through the Pretorio
a giant upon earth
and reels and falters in his gait
till he dwindles to flâneur
with an ashplant
looking for earth bare earth
to draw a sign
thus

I want to take Kaempffer
till I taste the *k*
its little wrinkly
– oh that wrinkly muscle
on the pearly stile
then the soft mallowy plush after

I'll be poor Poldy
looking up your thighs
to that unimaginable virgin cunt
virgin most powerful
virgin most merciful
poor Poldy with his unused dick
stiff as a stick
and stuffed with the obvious
cuckoo
cuckoo
and then I'll become
Henry Flower Esq
a languid floating flower
or I'll be a man with a spade
digging away at the beginning
a man on Sandymount Strand
who has discovered
un coche ensablé
oh those heavy heavy sands
they're language
silted here by wind and tide
and am I walking into eternity
along Sandymount Strand
with you know which sweet William?
cursh crack cursh crick
– Dr Kaempffer

the soles of my feet crunch the bladderwrack
and that housemaid's full bladder
bops back into my head
obsessive vulgar tender
my Poldy
then I imagine
the *pick pick pick stut pick*
as my Telemachia is typed
in a grain warehouse
under mountains as ample
as Agamemnon's tent
all my writing turning *spick!* into print
on a stiff black highstanding
Jewish machine
it comes out like ticker tapes or telegrams
angry but irenic
so I dream of a building
with lifts and doors and windows
or a well in the desert
my wadi my palmgrove
where the leaves clatter
stiffly like swords
or the beaks of watching birds
and water comes mushing to the surface
but not definitely not
like the jeddo on Lac Léman

as Gerty MacDowell
meets Gertrude Kaempffer
under the tent
of an epic fiction
so Peter Ivanovitch
meets Mikhail Bakunin

on the long road from Lugano to Locarno
in May 1870
– no tea in Locarno he complains
definitely no tea parties either
and no society
least not in the bourgeois sense of the word
but after Geneva
after Calvin's desert
this is Italy
in all her welcoming warmth and beauty
her primitive pleasantly childish
simplicity
now Bakunin finds a friend
a gunsmith Angelo Bettoli
because the passion for destruction
is also a creative passion
– Bakunin translates
three pages of Marx a day
in a villa by the lake
on the road between Locarno
and Bellinzona
when he dies a lawyer writes
on the death certificate
Michel de Bakounine
rentier
now Bakunin and Konrad
can fight it out
because this is the frontier
between battlefield and fountain
between the captain's tent
and the thymy mountain

welcome to them both

Konrad takes charge
and organizes the railway connections
between St Petersburg
– the most abstract and intentional
city in the world
and Geneva
– it's abstract too
a student tosses a bomb at Plehve
who becomes blood and brains
steaming on a snowy street
the same student lies on a bed
which he believes is the bed of a friend
almost a cradle
like a swallow's nest
and as he lies on this bed
he puts the backs of his hands
over his eyes
– why?
the believed the unproved friend
who is also a student
dreams the great autocrat of the future
his goggle eyes
and stubby fingers
that secrete fat
and stain any page he touches
while under or above
whatever is hot oily mammoth cruel
there is the cold the clean the petite the meek

now he looks at the lamp
the extinguished beacon of his labours
a cold object of brass and porcelain
amongst the scattered pages of his notes

and small piles of books
– a mere litter of blackened paper
– dead matter –
without significance or interest

perhaps life is just this?
– a dream and a fear
by a lake
whose precise orderly and welltodo beauty
must have been attractive
to the unromantic imagination of a businessman
– in that café at Évian
yes three years after they brought Ben Bella
across the lake in a helicopter
– in that café at Évian – Évian-les-Bains –
I watched this surly couple at a table
though we were – just – in France
I thought that couple was Swiss
surly and bored with each other
sitting wide apart at the slatted table
a couple whose fate was made secure
from the cradle to the grave
by the perfected mechanism
of democratic institutions
in a republic that could almost be held
in the palm of one's hand
the whole view
with the harbour jetties of white stone
underlining lividly
the dark front of the town to the left
and the expanding space of water to the right
with promontories – jutting promontories –
of no particular character

it had the uninspiring the glistening fixity
of some new – new banal and expensive –
Hôtel du Lac poster

the double agent
turns his back on the town with contempt
how odious – oppressively odious – it is
in its unsuggestive finish
the very perfection of mediocrity
attained at last
– at last attained –
after centuries of toil and culture
it's as though
each and every idea
can be seen reflected
on the eyes
so the ageing revolutionary
Madame de S
is an ancient painted mummy
with unfathomable eyes
and Laspara his eyes alone
– almondshaped and brown –
are too big
with the whites slightly bloodshot
by much penlabour under a lamp
the obscure celebrity of the tiny man
is well known – polyglot
of unknown parentage
and indefinite nationality
– anarchist with a pedantic
and ferocious temperament
– as I copy these words I wonder

did he believe this racial idiocy?
or just feed it to his readers?

*

the first parcel
is a small brown paper parcel
that holds a waste of roubles
the silly Kolya stole from his father's desk
to aid the heroic silent student's escape
– flung out of the St Petersburg express
it lies on the great plain of snow
like a host placed on an autocrat's tongue
by a disgraced priest
R – that student –
will enter a room
three days later
in the villa between Locarno
and Bellinzona
where Peter Ivanovitch
in his dressing-gown
and dark glasses
like an enormous blind teacher
looks at a map of Russia
à la clarté des lampes
with the tiny Laspara
– a bear and a flea
they perform their silent circus act
in a dusty cold room
dirty and cussed
as I an old teacher of languages
an Englishman but expatriate
feel that the old settled Europe
has been taken to a secret circus

a dumbshow
with a single spotlight
and that outdoor/indoor
sense of unsettled space
an abstract odour
that belongs
– if *belongs* is the right word
to almost any Irish play
– did I mention
dozing at the ringside
the fat heavy bulk of Nekator
slayer of spies and gendarmes?
can I even explain
the dusty fleshiness of any circus
the glitter in the dust
– glitter of pleasure dark tomb
and the whip cracking?
as I ascended the Rue des Philosophes
I recalled how Helvétius
turned each and every idea
into sensation
– Helvétius Helvetia
how jogtrot how boring
and then in a quick cold terror
I ask myself
why and when am I living here?
the bars of gold
in the vaults of Crédit Suisse
like that bar of human soap
in the drogheria in Bolzano
complacent silent secretive
the look of buildings
that are hiding something

buildings whose windows
somehow never meet your eye
buildings that know no mob
will ever burn them
– each bank is a stoneclad tank
quite massively sure of itself

from the windows of a building
– a building with terraces and balconies
came the banal sound of hotel music
before the low mean portals of the casino
two red posters blazed
under the electric lamps
with a cheap provincial effect
– and the emptiness of the quays
the desert aspect of the streets
had an air of hypocritical respectability
and of inexpressible dreariness
– not the plume of the jet d'eau the jeddo
its workings yet another
state secret
not that stately plume
can bring joy to this city

she assented to my reasoning
and we crossed diagonally
the Place du Théâtre
– of course I mean we crossed
the Place du Théâtre
diagonally
the first is a scruple that comes
from placing French before my native English
– if it is native English
for I too like Laspara

am a rootless wraith
as rootless as he who writes me
– with its slabs of stone
the Place was bluish grey
under the electric light
and the lonely equestrian statue
it stood all black in the middle
– now what I describe I mean
but does it describe my meaning?
at last we turned
from the Rue de Carouge
– jogtrot that name
cuckoo cuckoo
like Helvétius Helvetia
or the constant sight
of the jeddo
in this cold city pastoral
where the sound of a timbrel
is invisible unheard
the sturdy creak of a tumbril
softened into nothing
and I feel like a tray
of old postcards in a junk shop
– no gloss no sebum
just dust and baldness

I felt profoundly
my European remoteness
– let me hitch it back
– I felt my European remoteness
profoundly
fated to be a spectator
now I use my own language

at one remove
like an itinerant writer
with a prewar accent
out of date clothes
and a habit of saying *good show!*

Natalka unties her black veil
the veil drops from her fingers
– think how the text of the bible
has been glossed again and again
so again in this book of Europe
Natalka drops the veil from her fingers
the veil lies on the floor
between Natalka
and the heroic student
who is also a double agent
who after a day drinking tea
has imbibed a glass of milk
while staring at the bronze bust
of Jean Jacques Rousseau
where the icy river Arve
is bragging in its vault

the dropped black veil
lies on the floor between them
here I stand says the double agent
in the respectable and passionless abode
of democratic liberty
here I stand to tell you
I was given up to evil
– he snatches Natalka's veil
and runs out into the rainstorm
the thick fall of rain
envelops him sure like a luminous veil

in his room he wraps his journal
his confession
in Natalka's veil
as a Sikh might wrap the Granth
in a cloth or veil
now he runs through the luminous hailstorm
to confess to the conspirators
and give them this second parcel
– the notebook in the veil
while the other Laspara girl sits
dishevelled and languid
behind an enormous samovar
he remembers the taste of cream
in that glass of milk
and then Nekator
bursts both his eardrums
he runs back into the night
and wanders through pure storm
a silent night
like a tale told by an idiot
signifying nothing
only spectacle

– the rest is known
the silent tram that smashed his bones
the return
to a hut on the edge of some pongy village
he might have come from
and always Tekla
tending him like Antigone
who led Oedipus in his blindness
as far as the brink of the Chasm

when I returned
to that house on the Rue des Philosophes
Natalka was leaving for Russia
the pictures most of the furniture
had disappeared
she walked to the writingtable
now stripped of all the small objects
she'd used and made hers
– a mere piece of dead furniture
but a piece that contained something still living
then she took from a recess
a flat parcel which she brought to me

this was the third parcel
which contained the second parcel
which contained the first parcel
– the brownpaper parcel on the waste of snow
which became not the skin
tight on a packed slippy wad
of roubles
but the something else – not a thing –
that we call conscience
its agenbite
its inwit

and now we come back
to him looking at a lamp
– a lamp which had burnt itself out
it stood there
the extinguished beacon of his labours
a cold object of brass and porcelain
amongst the scattered pages of his notes
and small piles of books
– a mere litter of blackened paper

– dead matter –
without significance or interest

the burntout lamp
the blackened pages
the small piles of books
they both are and they are not
the Rue des Philosophes
the bust of Rousseau he stared at
while he drank that glass of milk
– they both are and they are not
Natalka's writing desk
with its parcel

in the end it comes down
to something being seen with the eyes
that now I recall
was also a black veil
– and it comes down also
to a cold smoky blackened lamp
and Natalka's trusting eyes
– her too trusting eyes
under that lifted veil

Locarno Three

A resort
on a kind of alpine lagoon
though it might be the runningboard
on a Lancia or Lagonda
even a Hispano-Suiza
– we could be talking Esperanto
as we try to put together
a pair of spats
floppy bowtie
a loudspeaker on a pole
or a tincan kicked
down a rocky hillside
maybe Chamberlain – Austen Chamberlain's
monocle too?
for he called the Treaty
'the sunshine of Locarno'
– he's locked into that name
and basks in its lost light

now it's two pails of water
balanced – that is located – on a plank
one called Jack the other Jill
unsteady as a tank
on a steep slope
it tips back-
wards and forwards
like a metronome ticking
a sound where something's

Austen Chamberlain was foreign secretary under Baldwin from 1924 to 1929. Devoted to the cause of peace, he played a prominent part in the discussions which led to the Locarno Treaties of 1925.

tacky almost sticking
like a boot kicking a bucket
full of sand

AUSTEN CHAMBERLAIN

A pen has a barrel
especially this black – this thick black –
secondhand Parker 51
that lies so snug
between my two fingers and thumb
till it becomes new again
in Austen's good right hand
as he signs the Treaty
on his birthday
                    British Delegation
                    Locarno
                    October 18th 1925
My dear Tyrell
at last the wonderful week is over
I have lived such days
and celebrated such a birthday
as is given no man
to rejoice in twice
and in the calm and the sunshine
of this Sunday morning
I try to disengage my feelings
from this moment's excitement
and to winnow the corn from the chaff
like Joseph Priestley
this Brummy Unitarian's son
aims to be
one of the great electricians of Europe

– a nice young man Bismarck said
a pity he's such a poor drinker
he always played the game Winston said
and he always lost it
clear as rock crystal Stevenson wrote
British to the core – precise
and angular like his features
the high collar the monocle that glittered
a slant rhyme with *Locarno*
the top hat he wore
in the Commons chamber
his stilted movements when he spoke
– flinging his arms out
striking his breast
drawing a horizontal line with one finger
then jabbing the air
like Don Quixote
tangled in a windmill
– a comic Victorian
wireless set anachronism
then a statesman
lifting us onto a mountain
where there's the first skinny nipple
of a cairn
warm rippling air
and a view of the promised land
in his huge open redleather limo
– his Leviathan he called it
this dispatch box on wheels
he was drawn through Locarno
like an archduke
– no round table in the Pretorio
so Austen had a long one sawn in half

to make an equal square
– it reminded Stresemann
of a butcher's block
or a table in a Bierkeller
while Briand dreamed
of a raft in the Atlantic
a solid Breton table
floating upside down
but to Austen
it was the circle squared
an idea as practical
as any of Crusoe's things
– his raft canoe candle
or big lump of beeswax
this world historical
table sawn table
was the thing itself
in the British Foreign Office
the final signing
took place in a suite of rooms
– mad ornate
like a maharajah's diningroom
in a Victorian countryhouse
where Austen is missing
the portrait of James II
– sent for cleaning sir

I did not want a blank space
on the other hand neither did I want
that unhappy Stuart looking down
on our signing
I therefore asked Lord Londonderry
to lend a portrait of Castlereagh

so the moving spirit
behind the Congress of Vienna
– too late I recalled Byron paired him
with *beast of prey* –
so the moving spirit like the plasm
that is the Spirit of the Years
blessed our signing of the Locarno Pact
but now I ask myself
the hand of history on my shoulder
was Castlereagh the right person?
was Londonderry?
Count Balbo's seaplanes
are skidding down Strangford Lough
Lady Londonderry is walking
through the gardens of Mount Stewart
with Hermann Goering
– yes the butcher Castlereagh
he was sheer bad luck

my dear Tyrell
I want to express – but how can I?
my deep gratitude
that I was allowed to take part in this
and next comes my wonder
at its complete simplicity
– so simple so natural so easy
only once did I hesitate
and nearly go wrong
– when I thought of leaving
the first draft to the French
but Lampson stout fellow
he saved my bacon
then after the signing

I walked to that little teashop under the arcade
– everyone – French Italian German –
everyone was cheering
it was like a marriage procession

at half past six we took our places
in that greatwindowed room
Hurst took the bound volume
of all the treaties we'd made there
and one by one each nation
signed the acte and initialled
the treaties to which
it was party
– thick pages like sailcloth
the pen a needle stitching
the canvas all through
with the thread of our languages

first Stresemann
in a few simple sentences
said Germany initialled
with a full sense of responsibility
– how neat the placing
of that little adjective!
and I knew then that Germany
was no longer a pariah
that might hunt with the Soviets
– next Briand
largehearted generous Briand
spoke sans peur et sans reproche
he thanked me
everyone clapped
I could hardly utter
my few broken words

– someone threw open the windows
Briand and Stresemann
they stepped onto the balcony
the crowd cheered
as they held up the Pact
Viens! said Briand
and I too showed myself
– how they cheered and cheered!
in the corridor
Briand took my wife
by both hands
and with tears in his eyes kept repeating
ah sans lui sans ton mari
je ne l'aurais jamais tenté
next moment Mussolini
the simplest and sincerest of men
when he isn't posing as dictator
– Mussolini had caught her hands in his
and covered them with kisses

the short drive home
again the cheers of the waiting crowd
my birthday dinner with the whole of my staff
– a real cake and candles
till I felt like a little child again

we took the yacht from Leghorn
– Mussolini came to wave us goodbye
imagine me
bathing two or three times a day
over the yacht's side
then barefooted in a cotton shirt
duck trousers a cholera belt
et plus rien!

then in Paris I exchanged
swallowtail and choker
for dinnerjacket and black tie
we heard Josephine Baker
oh we consumed champagne and poached eggs
while an Octoroon in purple glad rags
made us dance negro dances

I died within sight you say of failure
but I prefer to believe
that this was my Austerlitz
with neither the spit nor the kick
of gunfire
I never knew the name *Auschwitz*
– we'd travelled so far
that when I looked up into the sky
and saw the evening star
I was folded into the heart
of this one great goodness
and I was content to be another
lost – I won't say sheep –
more a lost mountain deer
fenced in some zoo
on the edge of a provincial town
where the air is sluggish
and the lights have failed
or else I belong
in that special circle of hell
no biographer ever visits
where every song
is past and not to come

the present Treaty
done in a single copy

will be deposited in the archives
of the League of Nations
and the secretary-general
will be requested to transmit
certified copies
to each of the high contracting parties
– this is our safety curtain
this is the last the final end
of the Great War
the circus is over

STRESEMANN

Why does Austen call me a Junker?
a proper Junker?
father owned a tavern
and brewed beer next door
I know all about mash kettles lauter tubs
hops malt grain spurging with hot liquor
I know how to darken beer with caramel
that malt is friable
and has a biscuity flavour
I know that *lager*
is also a storage cellar
not an estate with deer and horses
– he should call me bourgeois
fat heavy bald but a merry fellow
who refused court dress

Stresemann was a leading nationalist during the First World War.
Under the Weimar Republic, where he was briefly Chancellor, then
Foreign Minister, his views were more moderate, as he sought to
reduce the effect of the Treaty of Versailles. He was awarded a Nobel
Peace Prize in 1926.

– knee breeches and buckled shoes
when we signed the pact
under that damned portrait of Castlereagh
– he was a Junker
an Anglo-Irish Junker
– I've a dicky liver
and a short time left on this earth
but as I move through the press pack
with a Pilsner and a large cigar
I might be a foreign correspondent
as I tweak and stroke
and absorb rumours like a sponge
– I move
through the crowd
like oil through a lock
as I'm driven through the few streets
in an open Mercedes
with a black red and gold flag
– I'm a monarchist though
– Honour Freedom Fatherland
in that sense we champion
the republican black red and gold
wise policy
would have crowned the republic
with a constitutional sovereign
– the Kaiser's infant grandson
but the hole the void the absence
in our national life
means we cling to that wooden titan
Hindenburg who's thick
thick and dangerous
I dread what must fill the great gap
in the life of our nation

for the imagination's an aristocrat
– maybe that's why he calls me a Junker?
but I'm an aproned freemason
– what's Ludendorff say?
freemasons train their members
to be artificial Jews
– my wife is Jewish part Jewish
and I believe
we're not simple individuals
not drops of water skittering on a hot stove
– Woodrow Wilson
he was a Unitarian too
he didn't understand this
a scholarly recluse
he looked upon life from the outside
like a chemist in a lab
or a doctor prescribing
the exact form of government
all the peoples of Europe should enjoy

The Divine Architect of the world
    He didn't create mankind
as a uniform entity – rather He gave
    different blood to the different peoples,
the sacrament of their soul, their mother tongue.
    He gave them countries of different natures
for homesteads, but it cannot be the meaning
    of this divine order that we should use
the genius of our nation against the genius
    of the other and so turn back again and again
the great mission of civilization.

Gentlemen, peace is the emblem of this day, let the day –
when we signed the Treaty of Locarno – be a day sacred in

the annals of all Europe. To Germany and to France it
means: finished is that series of agonizing and bloody
encounters which have stained all the pages of European
history – in the past. Finished is that war between us.
Finished is the wearing throughout our countries of those
long veils of mourning for sorrows which can never be
appeased. No more wars ... away with rifles, machine
guns, cannons! room for arbitration and peace!

silence
men and women wept
c'est finie la guerre

BRIAND

As he was dying –
I mean bien sur while he was dying
Stresemann travelled to Paris
to meet Poincaré
he told the President I was afraid
of public opinion
– he was right of course
I never followed up our famous conversation at Thoiry
that long loving lunch we arrived at
like lovers incognito
under the dapplebright the dipply chestnuts
to discuss and to taste
the future of Europe our Europe
a footman brought the president a slip of paper

Aristide Briand (1862–1932), French statesman and politician. Many
times prime minister, he was the dominant voice in foreign policy in
the late 1920s. A strong supporter of the League of Nations, he
championed Franco-German reconciliation.

from Zandek
Stresemann's physician –
this conversation must end at once
his heart was all used up
– Hilferding his finance minister tested it
he had a duelling scar on his left cheek
kidney disease
a growth on his nose
that gave a sonorous ring to his voice
a finely cut mouth shapely nose watery bloated skin
small white delicate hands expressive eyes ruddy cheeks
a Greek freedom from superstition
we thought we were the Romans he told me
we turned out to be the Carthaginians
he'd a very marked directness
that was based
on a complete lack of selfdeception
his private hobby was Goethe the freemason
remember us
that eternal sunny lunch at Thoiry
when we tasted the promised land

 *

'suis noceur moi
the Joker in the pack
– put me in any suit
and I always win
but I quit Paris in August
– it's a hot tomb
and head out to sea
– Cap Finistère Belle Ile
no longer a nightbird
I'm a fulmar

riding the air by the cliff
you know there's a novel
– this is really quite odd
by that good calm little bourgeois
Jules Verne?
(I was at school with his son)
it's *Deux Ans de Vacances*
and there I am a schoolboy called Briant
who with his mates
wakes up one morning on a schooner
– a schooner sheathed in copper
called *The Sloughie*
there's no captain no crew
just ourselves alone
out on the Pacific
somewhere between New Zealand
and Tierra del Fuego
– we reef the sails
we plummet through storms
we land on an island
– sugar maples flamingoes
and an English skeleton
Verne gives us a good report
– 'these young boys
were self-reliant beyond their years'
but what he loves most
is a tree called a cow tree
its milky latex
we drank or turned into cheese
or wax candles
then I took a sabre to a jaguar
beat some pirates
and steered home at last

Verne worshipped that cow tree
– Brosinum utile
breadfruit and optimism
progress and steam ships
pig iron chucked from balloons
and never a problem
that couldn't be solved

I met Chamberlain
walking back from the arcade
with a new silk shawl
over his arm
– why?
– for my wife my dear Aristide
why you might've given it
to one of your poules!
I invited them both
to a tea party on the *Fiore d'Arancia*
– our purpose?
to steer that little steam yacht
to a certain place in the lake
where a certain kind of fish is found
Stresemann Chamberlain and I
we returned
with a huge invisible catch
one kind old pike
and a hundred young pike
– lovely slimy green pike
no one could see or eat
for in politics there are some things
no one can photograph
– movements of the spirit
the warmth and trust that nudged us

– three ancient pikes
badged with ancient sores
but healed – healed and wholesome
as we pretended
to be simply celebrating
Lady Chamberlain's birthday
with champagne and canapés
she and Frau Stresemann
that beautiful juive
how they added
to the gaiety of our nations
on board the good ship *Orange Blossom*
as for me
this old bachelor atheist
who is there to love me?
only when I speak to a crowd
am I redeemed like some comedian
but write my speeches down
they don't add up
their music is beyond print
– I can speak about peace
even bring tears to the eyes
of a German nationalist
otherwise I look and move
like an old flannel duster
chalky black tattery
some discarded rag
– a bat in owl light
my stooping shoulders
droopy moustache
a floppy jackdaw
un des chers corbeaux
délicieux

with untidy hair
always smoking and smiling
Corporal Caporal
mégot between my lips
– to my ear the voice I've trained
is a stony clatter
a chough's cry
knocking at a scree
a ricochet that's never real
never true
– but you say my voice
it's a deeptoned bell
caressing sensitive
tuned to the atmosphere
this noceur he never reads hates writing
prepares each speech in his head
– eyes blank like a bust
back taut and quivering legs
folded a dark shadow
across him
I'm a cat
le petit trou pincé comme un sou
indolent lightweight no
backbone just a voice
every phrase I try out on
an old illiterate peasant
Madame Martret
– I doze at meetings
a sleeper who listens
a lucky blackleather glove says Clemenceau
– a comforter –
my moustache still sticky with apéritifs
composed des bribes et des morceaux

this pilgrim of peace
he wanted a new equal Europe
its currency tight as a flightdeck

– it's only an olive seed we planted
but at least
nous avons parlé européen
we've spoken euro
how I love the good doctor Stresemann
as he walks unsteadily
down a staircase at the Quai d'Orsay
where the clocks are so high
you can't tell the time
– a stricken figure
under a blank clock
only weeks to live
how much poetry is about weapons
how little about peace

Aubusson carpet
long windows plane trees
shrubs
great lofty room
18th century panelling
Gobelin tapestries

I didn't do this lightly
or without reflection
but peace gentlemen
peace demands long service
peace must be grasped
and must never admit doubt
the German people
they aren't a compact block

an impenetrable square block
I saw a young man a soldier
blind his arms blown off
I imagined a future without peace

the shoe of Locarno
it'll gall it'll hurt sometimes
I imagine little crumbs of earth
as the olive pushes toward the sun

STRESEMANN 2

Augustus John is painting my portrait
he wants to talk but I won't let him
so D'Abernon the British Ambassador
whose portrait he's also painted talks to him
and together they design this allegory
Diplomacy Assisted by Art
it feels well like fake neoclassicism

we are now fighting for the immediate existence of the
German people
$1 = 3,760,000,000 marks

total war in the night and the mist
stretched your enemy out flat
but at dawn the landmass
was the spit on your dead father's face

the feast of Christmas and the Christmas tree has been
described as a German invention no festival in the course
of the year stands so near the kindly German heart as
Christmas the ancient German joy in light ours according
to Goethe is the race that struggles from darkness into
light

the night is dark about us and to many a friend of the Fatherland it will seem as though the lights of heaven are forever extinguished for the German people but as the stars are not engulfed because they do not shine on a dark night so also the moral order of the world is not suspended because we let this injustice pass over us

this socalled war guilt is a lie

in order that a dome may ultimately crown a building the mason must hew stone

born to see
set to watch
sworn to the tower
with the world I am pleased

Vladimir Ilyich

This journey is required
– here you must come face to face
with the petrific mace
which can never explain these rocks
– black diorite?
they're polished like ice
how can we have gone below the surface
to find only a deeper surface?
this is not a visit to a holy relic
it's not a pilgrimage
to gaze at a face and head
that look like a fossilized plastic egg
laid by a reptile before ever
history was invented
so he could pull
and throw its switches
like a signalman – secular
and intent – sleeves rolled up –
inside his glazed box
except this corpse
it's more like a bakelite plug
and has all the fascination
of ultimate bad taste
– the autoskeleton in its glass case
that once belonged to Jeremy Bentham
here he's raised up like a beach
or something that has rolled up
a raised beach
a bit of timber bale of rubber or an oil drum
tossed by we know what waves that rattle pebbles
like glass eyes clicking crutches or rubble

age upon age upon age
this terrible tunnel
is stuffed with zeks
drained and invisible
all heading down to
the lacu nigro
nemorumque tenebris
and what is laid out on this table
is one version of Frankenstein's monster
that's both institution and rebel
a bit of dreck
in an ordinary oddly civilian suit
a piece of ash fruit
– in what happens to happen
who or what makes the mistakes?

Somewhere to Get to

Car headlights
watch them sweep through the curtains
of a bedroom in a boardinghouse
somewhere in the Peaks the Derbyshire Peaks
– maybe it's not the first time
headlights have entered the little box of a poem
except the way they streak
they're like searchlights pushing through the night sky
but long years before bombs start to drain
down on cities factories railwaylines docks

the way the lights flatten bend refract\against the walls
is like a fly's wing magnified
and you're the dingy stranger incognito
with another alias – a Biggles
proud of his young life
who can fix the magneto
continue the war in the air
then retract
back into the night
and be hungry anonymous
like a prisoner or a spy
or the only English craftsman
– craftsman and artist
to join those male and female masons
as they strut their stuff
to build unser Bauhaus
against the huffy wolf
grey as the early Luftwaffe
who even now is padding towards his lair

on another peak
in what might be another country

the day bombs
started falling on England
you became eloquently dumb
became quite an important failure
as you left
the seas and forests of Europe
and no longer felt
the grab and pluck of its tides
as I must a downed airman
in a rubber dinghy that smells
strangely of wax as it rides
the slimy calm – no swell –
somewhere out on the North Sea
the German Ocean that may yet drown me
your onetime comrade
now a dinghy stranger who tells
you the language you process now
like chewing gum
has no kick no kick in it at all

Being and Time

After Hegel
this might be the next best key in the lock
– it despises loose or careless talk
like a poster in wartime
and locates the ecstatic
in the practical
– all that's vague will
not connect with Dasein
it alone cannot be touched
– that is moved by objects
or by other Daseins

from this it isn't much
to argue the intact
idea we must get over
the *in* of inclusion
a concept that's stacked
like chalk in a box
but unlike those dry sticks
– dry dusty sticks
you could never lick
it may survive
all the hard the percussive knocks

Clemenceau's Revenge

It may not mean a lot
to most people
but Trotsky's phrase – so risky
in 1927 –
for what would happen
nine ten years later
deep in Stalin's reign
when it's in trouble the new state
– that phrase *Clemenceau's revenge*
makes the dictator certain
that no one – and he means no one –
will ever be waiting in the wings
to replace him
– it's the main hinge
in the trapdoor
which is why Marshal Tukhachevsky
and so many many more
have just been arrested tried and shot
or simply arrested and shot

A Brush Painting

Some generals
or wouldbe generals
are taking a paper trip to China
– which is only to say
they've each ripped a leaf
from Napoleon's book
they know the future emperor
was an untiring reader
who studied *The Art of War*
by Sun Tzu
and wanted to write novels

Sun Tzu
a poet and strategist
he teaches us
that the elements of war are these
measurement of space
estimation of quantities
calculations
comparisons
chances of victory

he tells every general
go into emptiness
strike voids
bypass what he defends
hit him where he does not expect you
make devious routes the most direct
turn misfortune to advantage

when campaigning be swift as the wind
in leisurely march majestic as the forest

do not thwart an enemy returning homewards
and you must
to a surrounded enemy
always leave a strong
a golden bridge
because beasts at bay they fight desperately

if you attack cities
your strength will be exhausted

always survey the ground
carefully like a mapmaker
touch rock soil sand like a farmer
like a hunter smell marsh and forest
observe clouds sun dustcolumns rivers
read the wind glossing the reeds

ground may be classified
as accessible entrapping
indecisive constricted
precipitous and distant

know always
that speed is the essence of war
at first be shy – then
when you see an opening
swift as a hare

Strategy Again

In the coming war
Immanuel Kant's
more or less immortal intellect
will take up residence
in the office of a quantity surveyor
together they'll send tanks
and lorries in their thousands
to flatten the ragged no the raging spirit
of Joseph de Maistre

Schwarzwald oder Bauhaus

On a steep slope of a wide mountain valley
in the southern Black Forest
         at an elevation of 1150 metres
there stands a small ski hut
         a city dweller thinks
         that he has gone out among the people
         as soon as he condescends
         to have a long conversation
         with a peasant
but in the evening during a work break
         when I sit with the peasants by the fire
         or at the table in the Lord's corner
         we mostly say nothing at all
         we smoke our pipes in silence
now and again someone might say
         that the woodcutting in the forest
         is more or less over
         that last night a marten
         broke into the hen house
         and killed every chicken
         that someone's uncle has had a stroke
         that the weather'll turn soon
the inner relationship of my own work
         to the Black Forest and its people
         comes from a centurieslong
         and irreplaceable rootedness
         in the Alemannian Swabian soil
recently I got a second invitation to teach
         at the University of Berlin
on that occasion I left Freiburg
         and withdrew to the cabin

there I listened
to what the mountains and the forest
and the farmlands were saying
then I went to see an old friend a 75 year old farmer
he had read in the newspapers
about the call to Berlin
what would he say?
slowly he fixed the sure gaze of his clear eyes on mine
and keeping his mouth shut
he put his faithful
his thoughtful hand on my shoulder
ever so slightly he shook his head
that meant – absolutely no!
nation is the organic union of these millions
in a community of need bread and fate
all great worldshaking events
have been brought about
not by the written but the spoken word

*

the new goal
is dry assembly construction
that is the mass prefabrication
of residential buildings
– one orders a house
from the factory inventory
as one orders a pair of shoes
these are mail order houses
flatpacks
they arrive like presents

the standardization of our needs is manifest
the derby hat the bobbed hairdo

the tango jazz
coop products
presized stationery
and Liebig's meat products

our apartment house becomes a residence machine
modernity puts new building materials
at the disposal of our new housing
panels rods and rungs
of aluminum and duralumin
eubolite rubberoid torfoleum
eternite rolled glass and triplex plates
reinforced concrete glass bricks
Faenza pottery steel frames
concrete slabs and pillars
troilite galabite cellon
ripoline inanthracene colors
while in Esperanto
following the law of least resistance
we're designing an international language
in the standardized typography
of a traditionless script
typical standard wares
of international origin and uniformity
are the folding chair
the rolltop desk
the lightbulb
the bathtub
the portable gramophone
serial item
serial equipment
serial component
serial house

each one milled like a bullet
the standardized cultural product
is the hit tune
now we must consider
the aesthetics of the flat roof
because this catchword *flat roof*
it signifies only that the conscience
has become once more alert
– has once more become alert
to the original healthy meaning
of the roof
in this way one senses
all the way from a brass ashtray
to an apartment house
from a teapot
to a turbine factory
the completely new
the very intelligible unity
of manmade things
– independent
of dimension
and in contrast to all of nature
the will to cleanness clarity boldness
in design
has won a victory here
– a house of pure function

metal furniture
is part of modern space
it is styleless
the heavy
the pretentious upholstery
of a comfortable armchair

has been replaced
by tightly stretched fabric surfaces
and a few
easily dimensioned
springy
cylindrical brackets

one can only imagine
the inhabitant of Le Corbusier's houses
as a certain kind of intellectual
eccentric
unconcerned by sentiment
free to roam as he likes
and homeless
he prefers to live
in a nomad's tent
of concrete and glass
– hard materials true
but his house has not grown
out of the earth
isn't rooted weightily to it
not solid
but appears to have deigned
to land for a moment
like a colorful butterfly
– its wings flicker
and houses and buildings a thousand
miles away
fall flat
or push up
maybe they push up
like dawn mushrooms
but is it everyone's desire

to have a sleeping spot for the night
and fold his bed away come morning?
this doctrinaire design
gives the houses a strangely parched
pedantic flavor
and at the same time oddly
something provisional and barracklike
which robs them of a cheerful
heimlich charm
like Breuer's metal chairs
which are sitting machines
static engines
not chairs
they are without time
and have a kind
of constrained flair

let's put it as a schema

ecstatic objects	plain objects
many religious themes	few religious themes
the stifled object	the exploratory object
rhythmic	representative
arousing	engrossing (no analytic?)
excessive	rather strict purist
dynamic	static
loud	quiet
summary	sustained
obvious	obvious and enigmatic
close-range image	close-and-long-range image
forward moving	also flowing backward
large size	large size and many colored
monumental	miniature
warm	cool to cold

thick coloration	thin layer of color
roughened	smoothed dislodged
like uncut stone	like polished metal
work process preserved	work process effaced
leaving traces	pure objectification
expressive deformation of objects	harmonic cleansing of objects
rich in diagonals	rectangular to frame
often acute-angled	parallel
working against edges of image	fixed within edges of image
primitive	civilized

The Emigration of the Poets

(after Brecht)

Homer belonged nowhere
and Dante he'd to leave home
as for Tu Fu and Li Po
they did a flit through the smoke
– 30 million were no
more in those civil wars
while the high courts
tried stuff Euripides under the floor
and even Shakespeare got a gagging order
as he lay dying in Stratford
– Villon who wrote 'Les Pendus'
had visits from the Muse
and from the Beast
– i.e. the police
though at least Lucretius
was nicknamed *Le bien aimé*
and slipped away from Heim
just like Heine
– now watch me here Bertolt Brecht
I'm a pike
shtuck in this Danish thatch

The Night of the Long Knives

No matter the Führer is uncultured
he has Heidegger says
such beautiful such sculptured
hands – but these are dangerous days
and Röhm is cultic now is Hitler's
righthand man
so might not the philosopher
be talking in riddles
like one of our ancient warriors?

they chuck Röhm in the can
Hitler wavers
and yells at all the others
who're shot or hacked to pieces then
– they give Röhm ten minutes and a pistol
but he refuses to act the Roman
or else he stands his Grund
so they plug him in the brainpan
– when Herr Professor hears the sound
of killing on the airwaves
he looks over his shoulder and shivers

Voronezh

(after Akhamatova)

You walk on permafrost
in these streets
the town's silly and heavy
like a glass paperweight
stuck on a desk –
a wide steel one
glib as this pavement
I trimp on ice
the sledges skitter and slip
crows are crowding the poplars
and St Peter's of Voronezh
is an acidgreen dome
fizzing in the flecked light
the earth's stout as a bell –
it hums like that battle
on the Field of Snipes
Lord let each poplar
take the shape of a wineglass
and I'll make it ring
as though the priest's wed us
but that tin lamp
on the poet's table
was watched last night –
Judas and the Word
are stalking each other
through this scroggy town
where every line has three stresses
and only the one word *dark*

Ethiopia

i hope the organmen gas them to buggery
love evelyn

Chancellor Hitler's Speech

I reiterate here in broad outline
the indisputable facts
of Germany's fulfilment of the Treaties

the following armaments were destroyed

59000 guns and gun tubes
130000 machine guns
31000 trench mortars and tubes
6007000 rifles and carbines
243000 machinegun tubes
28000 gun chassis
4390 trench mortar stands
38750000 projectiles
16550000 hand and machine bombs
60400000 priming caps
491000000 rifle projectiles
335000 tons of cartridge cases
23515 tons of cartridge and shell cases
37600 tons of explosives
79000 munition gauges
212000 telephones
1072 flame throwers

in addition there were destroyed
sledges portable workshops
anti-aircraft guns
armoured cars
ammunition chests
helmet gasmasks

pertaining to the Luftwaffe
15714 chasers and bombing planes
27757 aeroplane motors

pertaining to the Fleet
26 battleships
4 armed ships for coastal defence
4 light cruisers
212 training and special ships
83 torpedo boats
315 submarines

the following equipment
was also destroyed
waggons of all descriptions
equipment for and against gas attacks
material used in projectiles and explosions
searchlights
direction finders
rangefinders and shell gauges

Germany on her part
has in almost complete
and total submission
paved the way to collective
collaboration among the nations
now I cite these facts
these hard facts
to justify the lives
and the cities that I
the modern Coriolanus
will soon lay waste

The Führer on Language

The English language
it lacks the ability to express
thoughts that surpass
the order of concrete things
– this means we Germans can think
and see more than what's square or round
but our language is damaged
by a poverty of vowel sounds
– we must do something about this

George the Fifth

In time for the morning papers
Lord Dawson of Penn
the king's doctor
announces 'we have done all we can
to stem the course of his disease
but now the King's life
is drawing peacefully to its close'
then knowing it doesn't matter if
some flunkey notices
he injects a mixture
of morphine and cocaine
into his jugular vein

Jarrow

Because the shipyard closed
the town went dead like dozed
timber or rusted iron
but maybe it was also Bede's swallow
– no his sparrow –
gave a flick to the myth
that echoes in the name *Jarrow?*
but the real rhyme
– that is the pith
the bony marrow
in this call it cultural primer
was with *harrow*
that dragged with it *hunger* and *hell*
joined to the juddering *j* of *justice*
the ploughshare's shudder
as its sock sliced
the earth making each marly furrow
chuck back that
slightly fatty that toolsmooth shine
the residue of all the generations
or of the knowledge they tholed
– work poverty solid energies
and drawn dole
as though the earth mocked – unwell –
them walking the strait and narrow
on this new Pilgrimage of Grace
through a dingy England of dusty mills
and welcoming church halls
their brows manly – furrowed –
as they turn their backs on the Tyne
that may soon be one with Nineveh and Tyre

while all the while
the North Sea waits for battleships
merchantmen more ships of the line

The Flax of Dream

I salute the great man across the Rhine, whose life symbol is the happy child.

They found the head-keeper sitting beside his hut under the larch trees, which had put forth bright-green shoots, and here and there the tiny reddish cones glowed on the knotted twigs. A sweet little whispering call came from above, and a female long-tailed tit flitted to her mate seeking for spiders in a pollard oak nearby. Old Bob was listening to their rapturous twitterings. His cap was off, for he loved the sunshine, and laid across his knee; a few silvery hairs, like the silk threads of a dandelion clock, still remained on his head. He did not wear a beard, nor was ever noticed to be clean-shaven, but always a thin white stubble grew on his face. The exposure to winds and rain tanned his cheeks till they were the colour of an acorn; under the tangled and drooping brows his pale blue eyes, misted by age, looked almost vacantly at the boys. The smell of hay and warm grass filled the space between them like a deep still breath, and he began to chant softly:

A swaam o' bees in May
Be worth a field o' hay
A swaam o' bees in Joo-un
Be worth a zilver spoo-un,
A swaam o' bees in Joo-lye
Bean't worth a fly.

London

FABER AND FABER LIMITED
24 Russell Square

Europe's Civil Wars

Generals don't in general shoot themselves. Let me rephrase that clumsy sentence. As a rule generals don't shoot themselves. After a failed coup yes. Or after a lost battle maybe. But these are acts of choice. They are not accidents.

It was at this point that General Balmes, the Military Governor, accidentally shot himself while he was at target practice. A clumsy fellow and a poor shot, he nevertheless managed to kill himself and give Franco an excuse to go to Las Palmas for his funeral. It was an absurd accident that in the excitable atmosphere of the time was rumoured to be either murder or suicide.

Just after midnight on 16–17 July, Franco was driven to the small island boat along with his wife and daughter. This was the first stage of a journey that would take him to supreme power in Spain.

All the Spanish civil wars must be seen as part of – engagements in – that longrunning European civil war which has lasted since the Renaissance. By idealizing the customs, religion, folklore of Spain before it became an industrialized country, those Spaniards who supported Franco sought to turn their pride into a political ideology. They insisted on a greater sense of personal dignity and rebuked material self-concern. They also showed an attraction to violence and to formless angry chaos or ancient night. A society built on the preservation of such attitudes is a type of fossil, an empty form which lacks any vital principle.

The Yellow Spot

We can see them still
lingering over a late lunch
in the Savoy Grill
though this time
it's the Ritz
– they're both in blue pinstripes
that look a shade chalky
– I've a hunch
that dry as dust texture
has to be exactly right
as they chew – Montgomery Belgion
a lightweight a nono who likes
the term *cathedratic*
as they chew Monty Belgion
and Tom Eliot
a knotty even a gristly
point – theology or politics –
no Tom says God is not a shout
in the street
most definitely not
– quite so says Monty
I know of course which Irish lout
said that – the same who put the Jew Bloom
inside his new green Jerusalem
of course Tom replies
I admire his well yes
his Jesuitical intelligence
but we must find some substitute
for that type of sense
it tends rather much to travel
though it could

of course be transported
to somewhere cold
– strange how everything comes back
to poor Coleridge's caves of ice
they're every bit as fated
as a railway track
– can I entice
you? says Monty reaching for the bottle
he completely fails to notice
a slight rictus of displeasure
on the face of his companion
who turns the subject to Byron
the church cat
suede shoes how awful
(does he not know I wear them
wonders Monty?)
– of course Arnold Tom says
was a mere savage
in a tone that's jaunty
the ever suave – or at least suede – Monty
says yes Arnold
might've been better on the stage
as a nigger minstrel

over coffee Monty
quite by accident singes
his winedark moustache
as a match manages to miss
his cigarette
– quick now
he puts it out
but for a long drawnout moment
like a breach of etiquette

they catch a bony a bristly pong
that might be a bad poem
or a worse song
trying to make a statement
– then not to embarrass
each other they play a favourite game
and try to come up – yes come up –
with a rhyme for *Ritz*
no not *Biarritz*
murmurs Tom if we test our wits
there must be some place some name
far away to the east
– maybe you can tell me what fits?

Hitler Enters the Rhineland

6 September 1936

Those sabots clocking the cobbles
in some Rhineland town
– they set an echo up
with *sabotage*
with the French language
its toltering bustle
on a dodgy field telephone
that keeps trying Locarno
then a phone somewhere in Britain
that won't answer
as the bulgy deputies gather
in the Opera the Kroll
Opera near the burntout Reichstag
while they fail the French and the British
– don't even try to stop
the march – has to be this name – of the Teuton
though hardly in hordes but faithful
to something in the mind of the nation
that is absolute and terrible
and will fight to the finish
caught up in its emotions
– pied piper again –
like bashed burst puncheons

Made Tongue-Tied

S/he has fled the ruins of the Bauhaus
and become an inner exile
– a refugee – in the new Reich
with a brandnew identity
as a sculptor who casts bronze figures
that don't look in the least political
like this standing figure of a Fräulein
in a bathing costume
her thighs crossed – crossed so tightly –
as if she needs but can't take a piss
while she pulls on her bathing cap
each now not delicate hand cupped
over her ears – either she hears no evil
or she's listening to a faroff electrical
pulse . . . it stabs and stammers
. . . *we will build the house*
again we'll shake its rafters
and make us all free

Spain

A salute is proof that our Brigade is
on its way from being a collection of
well-meaning amateurs to a steel
precision instrument for eliminating
Fascists.

500000 dead
no way is it over
no not yet as refugees
head in lines toward the border
– this group in a Magnum shot
marching with heads held high

¡No pasarán! ¡No pasarán!
that massed cry
survives defeat
like the fuse of a lark's song
as firing squads
take up position
in prison yards
the edge of a village
a deserted quarry
– almost innocent the way steam
rises from freshly spilt blood
as the Caudillo
like a cold heavy lizard
heaves his belly
and presses down like lead
so no one now can dream
of a new democracy
exact as a sunbeam
warming the mud
at the bottom of a well

P.O.U.M.
You think the pom pom of this
weapon would never give over.

Orwell in Hiding

Hotels had to report all guests to the police, so the three of them – McNair, Cottman, Orwell – spent another night hiding in the ruins of a church. Soviet agents had kidnapped and killed Andrés Nin, and George Kopp had been arrested. Orwell tried hard to get Kopp released. He went straight to the War Department in Barcelona and attempted to persuade the officials and army officers that Kopp should be set free. He failed. He and Eileen were very brave, foolhardy even, for they ran the risk of being rounded up themselves.

After their night in the ruined church, they spent the day walking the boulevards as if they were tourists. They bumped into several old comrades, who were also on the run or lying low. Among them was Willy Brandt, whom they tried to persuade to come to England with them. He said no. He was in despair at 'working man killing working man'. The cause was curdled, he could almost turn pacifist, except soon there would be war throughout Europe, throughout the whole world.

Eileen got papers and passports ready. She distributed the money she was holding for various I.L.P. members who were still at large, and met the three in the station at the last possible moment before the train left for France. Incredibly, the train had left early. So they hid out a third night and then made for the station again. They smiled and spoke cheerfully and confidently like happy tourists or delegates returning from a lively conference. The tension rather dimmed their talk as they crossed the frontier – their voices lunged and dropped, their bodies

stiffened. Then they were in France. They hugged each
other, shook their fists and cheered.

Nanking

This sticks in my gullet
but because I do not want to watch
as a Japanese soldier
sticks a bayonet
into a Chinese civilian
tied to a post
I reach for the zapper
caught between one guilt
and another

Understanding the Knot

A laboratory for the Luftwaffe
and the Wehrmacht
the Spanish theatre of war
is also studied by Dowding
who minute by minute
observes their tactics
– Schwerpunkt exact pressure
which he measures
like a scientist in a white coat
watching atomic
particles as they skip and jump
or drawing a graph
of sandfleas above a lump
of smelly bladderwrack
– he must understand the weapon
not the wound
study that abstract
adaptable weapon strategy
with a cold eye
and design diagrams
to maximize the dead
he must make a model
of this jittery chaos
this Iberian wreck
bloodbespattered vicious
but still a sideshow
still a provincial history
pushed to one side
– for the airman it's a race
to prove how wrong the French are
about matching tanks and infantry

as the lab clock ticks
and a knot tightens
that one day in the nick
of time
he'll know how to unpick

Stalin's Purges

Za chto? what for?
scrawled again and again on the walls
the walls and the doors
of cell after cell after cell
– as I drive through the townland of Eskra
in Co. Tyrone
I trigger *Iskra*
The Spark a Communist paper
one of the doors into hell
into the eyes of the tiger
and ask Kant's old question
what am I for?

As the train sluffed into Aachen
I could see a large shed
near the railway track
it was painted that dead
that glum green
you get on barns
and had a slanted roof
like a huge gnomon
or a ski slope
that was blank barren
– I was a few kilometres
from harm
and parched with hope
but as the brakes slurred
and the train stiffened
something struck
me in the look of that tin shack
a shadow
a dumb omen
I'd be turned back

Anschluss

One hot day that summer
we humped our rucksacks
through the suburbs of Vienna
as if the Old Man of the Sea
or a kitchen sink weighed on our backs
– or – horny and no angels
that heavy dream of girls

we drank a bottle of beer
and all we ate
was a tin of mackerel
for our dinner
or should I say *wor tea?*
– it was July 68
and fresh from the wee six
we were both anxious me and Neill
I can still remember
how there was something ominous
ominous and shrill in the air
as if we could just hear
far far away the measure
– heavy as our packs –
the jagged sound of a slow jig
and the name *Dollfuss*
or was it *Schuschnigg*?

Gellhorn's Story

Unanchored buoyant
so many smells tastes sensations
– timespots all of them –
my mind's pictures like windows
with their offers of presence
– these are my rations
though every so often
what just happens along I don't want
– now near the end
that's what frightens me
– the fact that a knowledge
might only be image
a thing I just see
then scrabble for dates
as if they could make it real

I'm in Gaylords Hotel
in Madrid – it's winter late
1937 at a guess
– Gaylords is the centre
of Soviet power
and E has been invited
to have drinks with Koltzov
I've tagged along
– that's my role –
to play his tough soft mate
and try not to bite

Koltzov was Stalin's ears and eyes
I liked him yes
– so confident so drôle
his talk witty and masterful

his blue suit beautifully
cut like his curly hair
his brown eyes quick but not cold
– for a long moment they catch me
and then I feel E's
watching and angry
– I turn – it's his shark face
the first time I've seen it
we drink some more vodka
and eat dabs of caviar
on real bread
I'm anxious and grateful
maybe guilty and spaced

later – a tad more than a year –
later I met Koltzov again
– he sat looking pained
on a stiff black leather chair
at the end of a long corridor
in Hradčany Castle
he'd been there for more
than four empty days
– he looked shrunken
not brilliant now – grey
and it was quite hopeless
waiting in that place
with a message for Beneš
who refused to receive him
and his message from Stalin
K showed me the text
– *we ask you Czechs*
to mobilize and fight
then the Soviet people

will throw in their weight
and stand at your side
Beneš he was a decent man
but bad for that time that place
he was all wrong
really he functioned as a spare limb
of the greater Satan
but K waiting with a manilla folder
was rebuffed by Beneš
who tried stay in the middle
between Stalin and Hitler
K here was a sad case
– now I have to say it –
he maybe held in his hands
the whole world order
or at least a better percussion
of action on action
as it was
one of history's loose ends
he waited and smoked
his way through what might have been
– some gnarled god could've designed
this national anteroom
and then forgotten it
dead glum oh real – much more than glum –
he and I walked back
down that long long
panelled corridor
out through a wicket gate and soon
we found a workers' canteen
in a side street oh it was wretched
an unsmiling woman
served us bowls of soup

– dull brown and greasy –
it was intimate and unclean
like eating in hospital
with a dying man
all we tasted was unhope
K kept glancing at a group
of men near the door
I knew beyond the room
something stank
and sweated like Minotaur
– it smelt of stale sacks

out on the street corner
there was a steel bollard
like one of its turds
– we shook hands there
for we knew the last time
K I heard was sent straight
to the Lubianka
– in the basement there's a special
– OK there was a special
narrow tiled corridor
one tile on that smooth floor
it touches a coiled spring
that releases a trigger
I hope that's how they killed him
– I'm not being hard
he wouldn't have known
wouldn't have expected that there
– K walks in my mind
ever and always
a poor used a failed thing
pushed beyond his own

his compelled crimes
– he too had his bit of paper
his useless bit of paper

A Constitutional Crisis?

The King wants to drive
– that is be chauffered slowly
(why do I glimpse *buggered*
in that verb *chauffered*?
it must be *Bognor* surely?
but that's another monarch
who might have gone there to die)
this one simply wants to go
like a simple
a wise and simple man
to Heston aerodrome
where he will try
and stutter out a speech of welcome
to Neville Chamberlain
on the tarmac

with due deference his secretary
– voice silky –
says your majesty I must advise
you that your majesty must not be seen
ever to take sides
(though you and I take them of course
and we take the right one
which must be peace with Herr Hitler)
but in the soul of this green
island nation
there could rise
a groan an ancient groan
that will shake
even smash the throne
if you are seen at Heston

– let him land
wave his piece of paper
then drive to the Palace
– you'll simply have to appear
with the Queen and PM on the balcony
which won't as it were look at all your choice

and there they stand
waving to the crowds and wearing
their smiles their appeasers'
smiles – fixed masks
as though they've just dressed
for a court ball
or have wafted briefly through the curtains
like three characters
in search of a play by Noel Coward
or else – else? –
they're like three serpents
three sleek eels
who've come crawling
over the wall
– no over the grass
into this popular garden
this sea just for the mo-
ment of shallow faces
– *shallow graves* I nearly wrote –
now watch these three pierrots
go through their routine
we are so bold
'cos we must keep hold
of our lovely state machine
when we're old bones
you'll still not groan

for on us you're keen
– your King and Queen
you're terribly terribly keen!

Le Sursis

In the heel of the hunt
Daladier returns from Munich
– paperfaced and defeatist
he knows he's helped wreck the Czechs
and his heart is heavy
as he lands at Le Bourget
expecting to be booed
by the crowds who wait
on the grass outside the arrivals gate
but when they cheer him loudly
he turns to Léger
and snarls *the cunts!*

Appeasement

Halifax the holy fox
he has a key
to the Palace garden
– often and often
we watch him unlock
the grey metal gate
– who gave him that key?
why his friend the King
but don't you get angry
it's much too late

Kristallnacht

Dieter Peetz tells me
'it was then and only then
that both my parents woke up
and decided to get out'
and I imagine him later
a young British soldier
firing a bren
gun at the enemy
then at the end one after another
interrogating SS prisoners
in his native German
– they're executed in alphabetical order
till the Cold War kicks in
was it at Schmidt or earlier
they stopped?
now with his red beret
he smiles and shouts
a good a dear man
a survivor
bashed but not broken
by all that history
oh God I share his anger
but how could I ever share it?
it's all that broken glass
the way it litters the streets
as though from the Reformation
to *Eikonoklastes*
to this night of murder theft danger
there's something complicit

Bushey Park

Their own worst enemies
silver birches ghost themselves
– they do so in winter
when their scribbly twigs look like hair
dishevelled hair
falling down but not quite getting there
– light and dark that particular mix
it doesn't belong though
not in this great park
where they might instead be a type of sallow
that grows – no ungrows –
along the banks of the Styx

those same birches in their hundred thousands
I saw them massed near Moscow
like a Grande Armée
sent through minefields
or plaintive in the snow
– I guess they're always sad trees
their bark's flakythin like skin
and for all I know
they share its pallor with the refugees

Nostalgia for the Future?

Zalosce is in the Ukraine
– this year 1938
it is one third Jewish
one third Ukrainian
and one third Polish
– its granaries like headless geese
are stuffed with grain
wheat dust skinks and twindles in the sun's
rays that'll also fall on brass
and on spit and on polish
– later oh much much later
in time of a new a postmodern
breakout of sealed nations
three Jews will remain
– three Jews fated
to live there with the last three Poles

Smart Sir Alec

On June twentyseventh
Dunglass – alias
Alec Douglas-Home
catches Harold Nicolson
in the lobby of the Commons
and takes him down
to his subterranean room
where they flap and chortle
like two smooth shades
like Manes in dark suits
Alec wants to know
about Harold's proposal
for a Manifesto of Peace
similar to Wilson's Fourteen Points
– but Dunglass oh much much later
is fixed ever and always
as he walks along Downing Street
carrying his gasmask
the way a magician
might carry his black tophat
a boyish almostsimper
on his cheeks
he likes the way *peace*
flaps its wings above *appease*
– he can't yet know
that – what twenty? years on
he and Dwight D. Eisenhower
will help rid the world
of Patrice Lumumba

Chaos Theory

(28/6/39)

When the Archduke's driver
took a wrong turning
in Sarajevo that sunny morning
twentyfive years back this very day
and the official limousine got stuck
in a narrow passageway
Gavrilo Princip couldn't believe his luck
he pulled out his tiny pistol
– neither Franz Ferdinand
nor his wife Sophie could duck
now we try to distil
from all the causes before our eyes
(or simply from Versailles
same day a mere twenty years back)
what tiny accident
– except it won't be an accident –
will put that ghost limo back on the road
– except it isn't even a road
on which we approach the critical state
where one or another incident
will begin the meltdown of all states
for this is the same date
they met in Versailles
to sign that – think of an adjective –
to sign that Treaty
and on the selfsame date
fifty-three years from now
– that is June 28th
1992

a little old man
corrupt near death
a former Resistance fighter
will descend from an airplane
in Sarajevo
among small arms and artillery
fire – but Europe will have forgotten
what it means this date
we will think only
that the President of France
Monsieur François Mitterrand
is in search of publicity

Kolyma

Scruffy shadows dirty shadows
from out the stink of a ditch
– except the only ditch
is a grey latrine
they're wrapped in torn rags
held together with string
they grip empty mess cans
and are bent shivering
under the crags
that glisten white with a tinge of blue
like loaves of sugar
that unfair that crystalline sheen
dropped into nowhere
– forked craychurs bare twigs
who broke the law
(one even dared claim Bunin
was a classic author)
these starveling bands
know that two three days
before the first snow
that subtle survivor
the dwarf cedar
will stretch out its five yard paws
quite suddenly on the ground
bend its black two-fist-thick trunk
and lie prone on the earth
throughout the long winter
– for what it's worth
they do not know
that Hermann Goering's hands
are shaped like the digging paws

of a badger
or that he reminds Lord Halifax
of the head gamekeeper
at Chatsworth
no these prisoners starving in frozen fact
who've been cut the rawest of raw
deals have other things on their minds

A Close-run Thing

Joseph Ball and Samuel Hoare
– both knights of the realm
both friends of Chamberlain
they're tapping Winston's telephone
then meeting with Horace Wilson
(a mere civil servant
he's England's uncrowned king)
– such people Winston talks to!
Jews pirates boyos
a raffish crowd
that belong under a heavy stone

Shirking the Camps

You write völkische Politik
early one morning
then get up from your desk
and take a hot shower
– you decide that you'll breakfast
at a café in the market
where you buy half a pound of Mocha
coffee ground for a cafetière
and a hard Swiss cheese
that agrees with your taste
– you decide this is quite European
but at this late hour
who can forgive the Swiss?
nobody but nobody loves them
then the answer comes back
your life is Swiss
– landlocked like a permanent dry dock
and so still so cool such a waste
of a good or at least pious
intention – how can you sing
a song of Belsen?
the Jews the queers the gypsies
pushed like forests of brushwood
into the furnace?
and not able to raise so much as a shout?
that chunk of Appenzeller
it tastes smoky on your tongue
but all you care about
is that its taste its slightly woody
tang is too obvious

Nazi–Soviet Pact

Stalin in a white jacket
with a raised collar
his face pitted
sebumglossy wrinkled
in that matey public smile
a maître d'hôtel might give
hard and shiny like polished tiles
– call it *greasy*
this smile that costs a packet
costs millions of lives
whole reservoirs tense with tears
as they sign away Poland
make it nulle part Noland
– Ribbentrop's smile is less easy
maybe he sees that October dawn
seven and a bit years down the line
when they'll fit his rope collar?

My Name

(after Akhmatova)

Tatar coarsegrained
it came from nowhere my name
and it sticks
aye sticks like a burr
to any disaster
– no it is disaster

August 39

In a house called Invergowrie
– Scotch baronial South Belfast
prosperous and Calvinist
she dreams an open boat
packed with a series
of starved figures
their ribcages bare as laths
– a hint somewhere in the story
(all dreams must tell a story)
that this has to do
with statistics or maths
– the sun is visible and hot
as an almost breeze makes ziggers
on the bluesmooth
surface of the ocean
that's as tight and sinister
as the phrase she'll bring back
from this involuntary journey
– *a dream and a fear*
for now she knows
that many miles from dry land
these ancient mariners
are entering their last sleep
they differ
from the corpse she saw last month
on the dissecting table
the corpse two students dressed
in an old overcoat
and played games with
as if it were a guy
ready for the bonfire

or as if it was a man full
of drink – but as the sea
is also known as the drink
there may be more to this than we think

not an oar but a gaff
– useless thing – leans in one rowlock
and that large hook
it spells out
all that she can see before her
and around and inside her
– a type of horror she hasn't met
with ever that's lodged in her now
like a message from father stamped
on her young mind
that six seven years later
she'll learn to understand
until years beyond
those newsreels of the camps
she hands her dream on
to her eldest son
who wonders if mere dreams
can weigh in the record
or for that matter can poems?

Albert Speer at Berchtesgaden

For that moment – a stretched one yes –
for that long moment
we saw the Northern Lights so bright so clear
they cast a double lustre on the coming night
(I need this bogus balance like an architrave
they're blocks of hollow stone my adjectives)
– the light was a good omen we guessed
except the sunset was a deep an unusual red
that covered all the rocks the Untersberg its pines
our whole bodies where we stood
more stiffly than we wanted
with what looked very like a coat of blood
as if nature even in the Führer's presence
wanted to embarrass him and us or
like a slip of the tongue a glitch
in a public speech or in a ceremony
nature was painting the entire world's
future history
as I the state architect – not
the state's architect note – as I
felt my soul creep and curl
up within itself desperate to hide
inside this mountain grave
which of course denied
that I could ever have a soul to hide
and all the while that mother bitch
she let a huge dumb fart right in our faces
– somewhere near Barbarossa's seat
we smelt the shit
smelt the dead herbs the twicebaked meat
the something else the vapoured grit

knowing we were already so steeped in blood
we couldn't turn the clock back
– in a soft trickle I watched the light
ebbing up a mountain track
like faeces
or an inkspill that made the whole process
about to be written out of this nether region
in red ink – dead
– the classic scrawl of chaos –
dead Roman capitals and severed heads
were what we saw and turned away from
– as I laid mine on the block I thought
when it's over this war between the nations
somehow I'll creep out from under it
and turn my back on everything I drew and taught
– there's a type of lizard that can survive
even total heat
to make its journey back from hell
and die alone unshriven or unshrived
a scaly animal
or bitpart actor
in the lift between the sixth and seventh floor
of a Knightsbridge hotel

Brilliant but Unsound

Rab says Winston
is a halfbreed American
now I know
he meant part native American
for in that heavy head I can
discern the ghost of Geronimo

Britain France Poland

It was ready our cavalry
they were oiled our guns
when between two flicks
of my cigarette
I Colonel Beck
(face like a sly debauchee)
said yes I accept
this guarantee
from our great and good Allies
of unconditional security
but once again I could see
the Christ of Nations
slouching up Calvary

Poland Invaded

We shall give the Germans not one button
our General's boast is best forgotten
as we sowed the heaths with our young men
no we shall not see their like again
we were the very last Romantics
– deeply foolish and heroic
whose forward defences lack of tanks
failed artillery obsolete planes
had to make way
for eleven cavalry brigades their sabres
sharp as they rode against Guderian's panzers
– I didn't choose this theme it stinks
it was like watching butterflies and ballet dancers
caught in the blades of a mowing machine
but because Hitler thought it'd be a local campaign
another Munich
– a bit of paper waved against the bullets' answer –
he was stunned by Britain's ultimatum
(he'd planned only to
move against her and France in 42)
maybe ashamed Ribbentrop stayed dumb
the former champagne salesman played for time
as the silence between them gathered and grew
sticky like glue
while Hitler cudgelled frown on frown
then said *Herr Brickendrop what now?*

Give Us This Day

PARLOURMAIDS AND
HOUSE-PARLOURMAIDS

THE KING AND QUEEN arm in arm, at Buckingham Palace last night

Hammond-Chambers-Borguis – On Sept. 1, 1939, Jubbulpore, India, to ELIZABETH, wife of DAVID HAMMOND-CHAMBERS-BORGUIS, K.O.S.B. – a daughter.

The realist's morning prayer
so Hegel says
(don't ask me where)
– that morning prayer
it is or has to be
the daily paper
– ie the light of day
the sun's rays
falling on its flimsy text
falling more like it on your reading
of its flimsy text
that is of course ephemeral
as well as – yes brother – prayerful
though not to an Emperor
on a white horse
not to that world soul
who crushed Prussia
like grapes in a winepress
on the plains of Jena
where maybe either he
or before him Luther
got this new day started?
though when all's done and said
there were – what? –
fifty thousand dead
they were the sticky bloody ball
booted into goal

know then
that these paper matins are
and are not history

Parliament
BRITAIN'S FIGHT TO SAVE
THE WORLD

[150

because your consciousness
– Hegel's thing –
your consciousness
is made up of that and this
plus this and that
– parlourmaids a son or daughter
smear of butter like an *um* or *ur*
(such rhotic fur)
bits of eggshell
like dandruff or clipped fingernails
that could be tiny scraps of flint
and then that smell –
almost – of burnt bone
above the toast crumbs
– they're really next
they live there stumm
these bits of dreck
small not wee
so very very small
like broken newsprint
– are they inside
or outside your head?
as you silently intone
this new day's chapter
of accidents
and make it *read*
– for *read* read *real*

GENERAL SIR EDMUND
IRONSIDE, the New Chief of
the Imperial General Staff
P. There was such a one, once. – T.

'STAND, CALM, FIRM, AND UNITED' – The King
broadcasting to the Empire from Buckingham Palace last night

WEST IRELAND – Lady with large house, own
demesne, invites correspondence anyone requiring
accommodation away from war zone. – Reid,
Carramore House, Curroy, Ballina, Mayo

Mr P. Tennyson Cole
In his book *Vanity Varnished*, he recounts his
vicissitudes in getting to and painting King Edward VIII

Male Poet Enlists

In form a punchbag
hanging from a rope
in a chilly gym
– it's the poem's shape
heavy and inert
until my gloved fist bangs
the bag and the hemp jerks
– this means I'm disciplined no lout
in this fenced camp
I can really put myself about
and make a *whap!* that shouts and sings
like a catspaw dusting the surface
of the sea – the Atlantic – with its fisty fuss
but the sarntmajor his mouth
full of muscle and cliché –
the sergeant takes the hump
and he shouts
call that a thump
you norrible little nancy boy no way
you'll make a fighting man
– like the rest of this shower you're a no hoper
– and your lines they don't even scan!

The Silver Sword

This will serve to induct
you into God's playground
or dip your hands in the blood
that flows from – it's a yuk
phrase keeps pushing into my mind –
that flows from the Christ of Nations

– at the age of seven
you are reading about Poland in 1940
– snow cabbage soup ersatz coffee railway lines
and helmeted soldiers
but you are spared the cattle trucks
as you try to see and catch the sound
of the writer's name *Serraillier*
– it glints like that tiny sword or a rapier
as if in 56 you could
know that injunction *write!*
must now and then rhyme with *fight!*

Norway

On the map a leaping hare
that proved elusive
we could have let her be
have let the hare sit
and stay neutral
like a strange creature
out of folklore
except this hare was running south
in agitation
the hounds were racing after it
– loud tinny dissonant
I could hear their cries
but as First Lord
of the Admiralty
I thought and said
we have provoked our mortal enemy
into making a strategic blunder
– my kapok phrases
were lumpy quite mistaken
we had put ourselves asunder
on Norway's fiords
and frozen mountains
her snowy endless fields
where we had neither snow
shoes nor skis
– those mountains acted like shields
as fighter bombers dropped
from skies they understood
my spirit sank low
maybe had I then the power
– had I been PM

we could have won
– to be honest I don't know
I saw those grey sea lanes
blocked by mines
I could out of someone's childhood hear
a crack a howl the pent
up ice split its noise the way wolves roar
all along the Gulf of Bothnia
I saw the snowstorm
over the battlefield of Pultova
and then a barren strand
the legend *his fate was destined*
I saw the gothic name Gällivare
and felt the threads of Lilliput
or recognized its umlaut
as two bulletholes
– Gällivare the Swedish mines that sent
by railway overland
to Narvik iron ore
for Germany – but was Narvik
a mistake for Larvik?
one north one south
who could be sure?
I felt like Gulliver
those ugly names stuffed in my mouth
as Quisling tried to make a ripple
through all his people
and this ramshackle war
fell like my star
I appointed General Hotblack
to take over
but walking back
to his club he collapsed

on the Duke of York's Steps
– his successor
flew straight to Scapa
but his plane dived
into the airfield
and he almost died
– we were unlucky
no we were stupid
we were scuppered

The Attack in the West

10/1/40 THE PLAN OF ATTACK

History lesson this – the heaven's cope
dome or belljar that contains
the whole mess – it's less
than a whole but it has a pattern
like an architect's drawing
– an explosion peaked
an unfinished scribbled
gothic Rotunda

– General Student tells his story
as if he wasn't responsible
as if he wasn't the teacher
and didn't send a staff major
from Münster to Bonn
with a large waterproof folder
that contained
the entire plan for the invasion
of Belgium Holland and France
– the major will go by train
to a meeting in Bonn
where they'll settle a few
quite unimportant details
in the invasion plan
– but the major misses his train
and is forced to catch a plane
– lifted up into the air
he imagines overtaking
that missed train
arriving early at the airbase
and perhaps risking a drink

– say a clear
not a bisongrass vodka?
– vodka crated from Poland
stacked high in the mess
but bad weather
the same bad weather that has
four five times stopped the attack
getting off the drawingboard
(the same drawingboard that the major
holds balanced on his knees)
– that icy
unpredictable wind
is even now bashing and lurching
the tiny tin plane
over the frozen Rhine
it loses height and becomes
a dodgy shadow
on the snowy fields of Belgium
then tries
to dip between two trees
that simply clip its wings
off so the plane
drops and crumps into the snow
like a gutted herring
where ten minutes later a Belgian soldier
runs unsteadily towards the major
and the pilot as they try to burn
sheet after sheet
of the typewritten plan of attack
– he arrests both men
and impounds the plan
– soon the Duke of Windsor
will leak the almost abstract existence

of those charred sheets in a safe
in a Belgian barracks
to the Nazi high command
– it seemed quite incredible
that just as in 1914
they planned to strike at France
through the centre of Belgium
and that knowing this the Belgians
would not invite us in
– they believed those dumb Belgians
that the plan was a plant
so did the French
ditto the Dutch
and if the plan was a plant
then there'd be no
trip back to the drawingboard
the plan was for real

THE MECHELEN INCIDENT

On the other hand
10/1/40 was a good day
at least by January standards
– a crisp cold clear day
when majors Reinberger and Hoenmanns
allowed their ME108 – or was it a 109?
yes a 109
when they allowed their Messerschmitt
– a virtual fighter – no light transport plane
made of cloth and string
– allowed their sturdy all-weather plane
to get blown across the Rhine
and a chunk of Holland

by an eastnortheast wind
– not a wind a mere breeze
of 9 to 12 knots
before they crashlanded
near the main road
between Lindenheuvel and Maastricht
where they tried and failed to set fire
to the courier pouches
with paper and damp sticks
behind some leafless bushes
– no soldier writing a report
will add an adjective that notices
the convenient bareness of those bushes
and no officer ever noted
that German High Command
had issued permanent orders
against sending secret papers by air
– an oversight that maybe rises
like a bituminous swelling egg
from out the deep pit of MI5
whose deputy director
Sir William Crocker
like his chum the governor –
Montagu Norman – of the Bank of England
has a secret line to Ribbentrop
who coos to the Queen of England
down cunning corridors
– yes it's that trope
corridors lined with smoky mirrors
no one will ever wipe

THE ATTACK

Imagine no imagine not
all those forts like snug ovens
like pot ovens ranged
all along the Maginot Line
concrete casseroles marmites
but tinpot really
and easy dodged
this Shield of France
this buckler
its electric trains
and underground cinemas
like a holiday village
stuffed with technicians
and incompetent officers
these permanent forts
they're torpid bodged
by a single halfbaked idea
for this is the siding
where Clemenceau's revenge
has at last been shunted
where it gathers moss
– the Ardennes forests Pétain said
personne ne peut pénétrer
so we need not fear
those deep dark forests
our line is long enough
like La Manche
the British Grand Fleet
or the Rock of Ages
– something mayhap be cooking
but not in this sector

where like an old man at stool
the squat god Terminus
keeps his lid on and waits
for the Germans – just
where we want them –
to attack through Belgium
except *Achtung! Panzer!* –
they know now more than any nation
about tanks
and will commune as always with the forest
then fight
the next not the last war
hence – stupid archaic word –
hence these concrete pipebowls
– warm gummy stuffed
their dream of comfort
like kapok hotels
énervé airless
altogether in the wrong place
the wrong time
with ten divisions
weak and bored
sitting out
the silence of the forests
and waiting patiently
to be attacked in this phoney
drôle de guerre

> Daladier fell off his horse
> Reynaud took over
> – each had a coarse
> upperclass lover

half our unit
was down with scabies
and the other half with crabs
so we gave each other
blue unction treatment
then stomped through a swamp
of yellow clay like Passchendaele
– yellow clay that stuck and dried
hard as a shell
though Gamelin he said
we'll go through Germany
comme un couteau dans le beurre
except the Seaforths they ran into
heavy continuous machinegun fire
– they were mown down like grass
we tried an orchard
then a field of wheat
a German plane came and quartered it
like a hen harrier
in this windless hot weather
almost no water no food
we kept still
and watched their motorcycle patrols
the flash of field glasses
like stammering lighthouses
at high noon
as dogs tied to the doors of deserted farms
howled old testament howls
swollenuddered cows bellowed
a French cavalryman
shot a line of horses
one by one
I knew we were finished then

I was in a ditch with Bristow and Adkins
when just the other side of the road
I saw forty fifty SS troops
– camouflagedress light machine guns
rifle bayonets and stick grenades
on their tunic collars
behind them
two halftrack light tanks
one soldier
small swine of a chap with a flat nose
shouted to the tank commander
who drove it up to the edge of the ditch
right towards us
– I thought they were going to crush us to death
but they ordered us out of the ditch
stripped us of our jackets steel helmets webbing
even our dog tags
then all in perfect English from Flatnose
they wanted to know
our unit our HQ the other
troops in that sector
– name rank and number
that's all we can state I said
they went crazy and kicked
and thumped us till we fell on the road
suddenly a British army truck
– officer truck with a canvas hood
over the cab
came roaring down the road
and stopped a few feet from us
the passenger an officer
and the driver they raised their arms
started to edge out of the cab

– they didn't have a chance
one trooper he blasted them back
with a burst of machinegun fire
the SS started clapping
then one chap he got a jerrycan
sploshed petrol over the bodies and the truck
then chucked a match
we were goners I knew
so I jumped through a gap in the hedge
got a stick grenade in the leg
but I ran on I
got away I got
to the longest beach in Europe
and went down like Aeneas
among the living shades
among twentypackets of Players
floating on the tide
the greybrown bloated faces
of drowned soldiers in overcoats
and packs – we lost
68111 killed wounded
missing or taken prisoner
63879 vehicles
2472 guns
76000 tons of ammunition
500000 tons of stores and supplies
c'est bien beau que les Britanniques
pouvaient ficher le camp
nous n'avions pas le luxe
ils sont retournés chez eux en héros
nous sommes revenus à l'ignominie
à une débacle belle et bien énorme
La France aimerait juste nous oublier

nous étions comme des mots étrangers
des mots qui essaient de pénétrer dans la langue
nous étions comme des faux-monnayeurs
ou des gens véreux personne n'aime plus
but the weather was with us
– neither rough seas nor a clear sky
the sea smooth under cloud cover
– licked by haars seamist fog
the flotilla came crossing the Channel
a golden bridge was it?
or Hitler's remembered fear
of thick Flanders mud?
no one for definite knows
though one thing's certain
our stranded army
was the Appeasers' dream come true
– if it stayed there stuck
we must sue for peace
and Churchill must fall
MOSLEY FREED CHURCHILL IN THE TOWER
worse and worse the headlines
I manned a lifeboat out of Dover
it was like painting a wall
in the middle of a battle
– there was a job to do
so I did it
me I was on a forced march to Germany
when my wound played up
I stumbled so they
bayonetted me in a ditch
and left me to rot
109s kept diving
hosing the beach

one chap had a brengun on a tripod
they sliced him in half
one soldier came ashore
playing a piano accordion
another carried a collie dog
another a dartboard
those oily bearded faces
helmets blasted open like metal cabbages
ragged mackintoshes battered caps
an army of ghost crabs
edging out of the water
lonely on our island
we felt free again
quite serenely cheerful
like young men
eyeing the girls
at some thé dansant
in a seaside town
we became ourselves again
ourselves alone

into the mosaic of victory
I lay a pattern piece
my only son
into thy hands

Churchill

10/5/40

Telegrams ribbed cardboard boxes of telegrams
from dawn on they spat and kicked
– klotzen nicht kleckern
into the Admiralty the War
and the Foreign Office
– the Germans had struck
their long awaited blow
now the whole huge movement
of that army I had warned against
all my parched years in the wilderness
was pushing and crushing
all that stood in its path

they said Winston you must preserve
a complete why an absolute
a jammy silence
– if you speak first
then you're lost
– at eleven that morning
I was again summoned to Downing Street
by the prime minister
and there once again
I found Halifax had preceded me
like a secondguesser
or an ample
familiar ghost
robed in ermine
– or was it Chamberlain's ghost
his ghost to be
I saw in the far corner

of that drawingroom chill and fixed
like a stage set?
– it was a trap
this arranged meeting
between a dying man
a former viceroy
and myself
– the powers in the land
they all wanted Lord
Safe Pair of Hands Halifax
– the King Chamberlain Attlee
all behind him while I
was a reckless adventurer
strapped by the Dardanelles
the Duke of Windsor
and Norway
– how could I break their will?
this was a trap for a Trappist
unless – ho you've guessed it –
I kept my corny trap shut
a silent invisible man
or abstract ghost
though I felt more like a Michelin man
snug in my blubber
of tubby silence
– then Chamberlain spoke
I said nothing twice
like a monk trying to hear
the sound of one hand clapping
I underlined nothing with silence
I dotted the *i* in *nothing*
with silence then gazed
into the almost ostentatious

rubber tyre of its *o*
oh no
this was a silence longer
than the two minutes we observe
on Armistice Day
a moment of more than quiet
but crowded with all those shades
standing proud above their broken bodies
out of time and in time too
a moment that first chilled
to absolute zero
then built to the knowledge
that the whole of my life
had brought me like Aeneas
to this one glimpse of the Latian shore
– Behold the Lord the Lord of hosts
shall lop the bough with terror
and the high one of stature shall be hewed down
and the haughty shall be humbled
– was I the prophet
or did the prophet speak against me?
it was then I felt
– felt unbearable on my shoulders
the burden of the desert
the burden of the desert of the sea
and Babylon fallen fallen
but still I wrapped myself
in the mummy cloth of my silence
while the silence in the room
held like a high dam
– then Halifax spoke
– no dam now a bridge
over a clear bubbling stream

– as a peer
I am of course out of the House of Commons
upon whose confidence the life
of each and every government depends
– I cannot therefore
be prime minister
– at six I went to the Palace
and at three that morning
the prophet vindicated
sank gratefully into his bed

Or in a Soft-skinned Vehicle

Samson in the temple
is what it feels like
– hard and hexagonal
like a pillbox
on a wet field
its still shiny sides
taking the *pok pok pok*
of machinegun fire
from their cramped or slimy hides
on the edge of the woods
but now we're observed
the way we watched birdlife
in another time
– soon the big guns'll arrive
and we'll fight to the finish
– be the last of the British

here and now is simple laidout
tank tracks on muddy ground
their marks spilt letters manilla envelopes
that lead to a pillarbox
– no they point to a whole people
a whole people and more
who're stuffed inside
this exposed island hideout
like prisoners waiting to die
in a completely new season

we are the shield
in our mouths the taste
– a taste that's so sore –
of raked cinders and unhope

our nation may soon go down
among the dead men of Europe
– Belgium France Holland and Poland
as we stand with our beaten soldiers
on that long shore
stand like ghosts
like sighs
strafed by the Luftwaffe
waiting for waftage

And Let My Lamp

Our local post office
is always a village
even deep in the city
as we pay for postage
it feels like the country
it also feels as if
the state can protect us
with its stamps rationbooks coupons
its wireless and dog licences
– as though we're queuing in a tiny nissen
hut made of cardboard and brown paper
or climbing a papiermâché tower
that isn't the least bit lonely
and whose light is steady

Boca di Inferno

A state secret I want to unlock
is Hitler's wedding present to the Duke
and Duchess of Windsor – a little gold box
that may by some fluke
have survived in a locked archive
where we might read the inscription
that looks forward to his restoration
zu seinem rechtmäßigen Thron
– his rightful throne
but we may never know why Rudolf Hess
flew all the way to Lisbon
– never know exactly but we can guess
that Victor/Hess told Willi/Duke
of the plan to fly him to Germany
where as a spy he would secretly
be awarded the Iron Cross
– yes the Iron Cross First Class
which would one day soon be welded to his crown

Trotsky

An adobe ranch was my procreant cradle
my swallow's nest then my Alamo
when he – when Ramón Mercader
smashed that ice pick
into my skull
(it was like I'd been hit
by a heavy truck
– or been brained by a dustbin
yes you caught that speech
when I bashed when I wrecked the Mensheviks
in the Petersburg Soviet
way way back)
history I know
was our highnoon metaphor
was the actions of a god
we couldn't believe in
our portable predictable altar
but the generations
that've trod have trod have trod
we trod on them until most
of us were pushed or trodden down

as I slowly went west
in my study at Coyoacán
– always the hard heat of Mexico
I had time – no not to make my peace
but to contemplate the vast
extent of my failure
– it looked like the bodies
of those Kronstadt sailors
lying on the snow

Luftmensch

Tougher terser
yet somehow more abstract
than *rootless intellectual*
the term *Luftmensch*
(it's antisemitic)
could be brushed onto Walter Benjamin
who stayed in cheap hotels
or rented a flat
then chucked it in
when those four recognized walls
began to feel like home
then for short always exact
periods he dossed down with friends

after he fled Berlin
the Bibliothèque Nationale
was the only place
he allowed himself to feel at home in
it couldn't be a sanctuary
for it gave him only
a brief a passing illusion
of safety that ended
with the German occupation
so the Luftmensch left for Spain

he was turned back
he knew his fate
— a cartoon rat
in a cartoon sack —
so he killed himself
in a smelly hotel
near the Spanish frontier

it's really too facile
to see this as a symbol
of his unhoused writings
– OK my comments shine
with a perhaps predictable
reflection of the *I* who writes
what you happen to be reading
but do not wholly reject
my placing of this haunted
hunted figure
on that frontier

The Invasion Handbook

South-East: Lowlands
North, West and South-West: hilly country
North and Scotland: mountains and moors

Hinchley-Cook wears fat, hornrimmed glasses. He is robust, fresh-faced, appears to be good-natured by temperament and speaks German fluently in a mixture of dialects from Saxony and Hamburg.

The English, especially those who inhabit cities, read papers in the mornings only.

England is the country of Freemasonry. English priests of the Enlightenment era were the foundation on which the ideology called Freemasonry was built.

There are about 150 Public Schools. In social standing the most distinguished are Eton, Harrow and Winchester, Rugby, Charterhouse, Marlborough, Clifton, etc. Hardly 1% of all children currently go to a Public School, but they will eventually occupy about 80% of all important posts in politics and the civil service. These Public Schools
  they are in fact private – are the schools of the English upper class, and to have attended one of these schools is forever the pride of any Englishman who is a member of that class. Fathers often register their children at birth with the Public School that they had previously attended (Eton College is booked out until 1949).

The historical significance of Freemasonry, which spread from England to the Continent, is the advancement of Jewish emancipation in Europe. That emancipation arose from the intellectual and political heritage of the Free-masons.

The Jews believed they were God's chosen people on earth and this Puritan tradition led the English to regard themselves as the chosen people of this world.

The gold and diamond industries are almost entirely dominated by Jews.

If we really want to understand the structural essence of British intelligence, we have to free ourselves from conventional ideas of strict and careful organization, from the particularly German need for precise detail, discrimination and definition. Nobody can truthfully say that the secret service is organized in such and such a way, is located here or there, or employs this or that person who performs this or that task. The contradictory, the frequently arbitrary characteristics of the English, of which their language is an example, are also conspicuous here, where the English have achieved mastery through tradition and experience, supported by certain attributes of their national character – unscrupulousness, self-discipline, cool calculation and ruthless action.

Special Wanted List
Abercrombie, Lascelles, 9.1.81, Prof. u. Dichter, wohnh. Oxford, Merton College, RSHA VI G.1
Zweig, Stefan, Dr., 28.11.81 Wien (Jude), Schriftsteller, Emigrant, London W.1, 49 Hallam Street, RSHA II B2, IIB5, VI G1

Two thousand names, excluding David Lloyd George and George Bernard Shaw.

Slides of persons to arrest

It is likely that the Duke of Windsor will be restored to the throne, and that the prime minister will be replaced with Sir Oswald Mosley who is in prison currently. Henry Williamson, who is author of *The Flax of Dream and Other Poems*, (he is in prison also) will replace the Poet Laureate to the English Court, John Masefield.

Battle of Britain

Our master Mitchell is in his office
a hand under his head
a fly on the plateglass window
he doesn't hear
stubby shortlegged and determined
like his slow cancer
– quiet the teabreak shut the door
his mind needs silence
as he squares to this problem
then dodges back and around
– one accurate gun in the nose
or four on each wing?
is a pilot a huntsman
an ace an aristo?
his answer is *no*
– does he want to design then
a flying shotgun?
his answer is *yes*
as his mind moves across paper
– poolsmooth paper shiny
as the North Sea that might
be the German Ocean again
as he designs the template
for his temperate fighter
– a small clean fuselage
slim curved wings
a perfect compromise
with all the qualities
required of a fighter
it's British Bauhaus this plane
– british bauhaus

clement oddly gentle
with its so straightforward
stressed skin design
an allmetal monocoque
with a flushriveted light
alloy skin – Hercules' – *Hercules's*
worldwielding shoulders

a lovely feeling
my Spit's new gluey controls
as the Junkers
is slowly hauled into my sights
– then thumb down hard on the trigger
such smooth shudders
like farting through silk
as my eight guns blast out
and his tail
folds slowly back on the wings
– huge smoke and flash of flame
the squirt from my flying sawnoff shotgun
had chopped him in half
– one parachute blossomed
and I felt almost tender
as though it was a child's soft skull
or a dandelion clock
though we were the lions
and they the eagles
– *another cokernut!* I shouted
it's cardboard lingo we talk
one must never shoot a line
– laconic nonchalant spry indifferent
we clip our words like bus tickets
matteroffactly

we know
we're not in the navy
not in those terrible convoys
– week upon week
of cold and fear and storm
way out on the treacherous
swaying deep
like molten cold metal
while we rise up
higher still and higher
in our clouds of fire
rise and sing like larks
from our hidden messes
– snug messes snug beds
we deal our cards out fast
sweep the table
or plunge quickly
like flies or hairs
chucked in the fire
where they blaze like luck
– bad luck's good luck
compared with the deep desolate
the open sea
– remnants of Luftwaffe Staffels
still circled above us like ash
the ack ack was brutal
buckets of it everywhere
like lumps of coal thrown up
– the first week in September
we lost – add it up –
a squadron each day
and if Hitler hadn't bombed London
because Churchill bombed Berlin

what would have happened?
London took it
we gave it back
and Stuffy Dowding he
loved us like daddy
– why they shoved him out
no one knows to this day
look at it this way
August 24
the Luftwaffe mounts a single night raid
on London
bomb Berlin! Churchill orders
September 7 they shift
and attack London by day
1000 planes on a tenmile front
September 15
is Goering's final effort
two days later Hitler postpones
Operation Sealion
– the Battle of Britain is over
the war goes on

patched and peeled
a skin cento
– or skin centone
as Jed Jenkins in his eerie
best Eyetalian'd say
– yes you've guessed it
that shit Hillary
is flying his kite
– I mean my face in gummy tatters
its different types of skin
almost like different brands

stretched layers that grow
like forced rhubarb
rhubarb rubbed scrubbed dubbed
like a white stone step
– this is Richard calling
Richurd
has broken out of the closed language
we use in the mess
and taken it with him
into so many lovely beds
– see him see me
an orangutan in facegauze
no central ridge in my new upper lip
as I apply my tongue
– my tongue tip
to Merle Oberon's clitoris
– it's no dream this
though I of course am part
of Europe's nightmare
like the sad monster
Mary Godwin hatched
in that château in the Alps
my patches and peels
are like that Dutchman's who squatted
on a windowsill
above an earth that for some politely
churlish reason
is jampacked with merds not turds
though both of them go with *Richard*
Richard whose eyes are coated
with a thick layer of gentian violet
his fingers extended like witches' claws
his body hung loosely in straps

in the tin hospital
where the plastic surgeon grates and shaves
the skin on his bum
the skin on his belly

they were just about the nicest bunch of men
I can see Dixie
— diminutive desperately keen and nineteen
Bubble Waterson
his shortcropped hair and open face
— from this flight Don MacDonald did not return
— from this flight Larry Cunningham did not return
— from this flight Bubble Waterson did not return

every Spitfire has a white enamel
undercarriage plug
exactly like a lavatory plug
— the sight of it
always pulls the rug out
from under me as I see
us dropping through the state's drains
which by a commodious
recirculation turns us up
and back as heroes young men
against the high stretched blue sky
of Kent or Lincolnshire
— every Spitfire
will have smoke stains
all along the leading edges of its wings
and it will look in flight
almost innocent almost gentle
a fixedwing creature
metal ephemerid
that's just hopped

off the drawingboard
for its 75 minutes in the air
where it faces
yellownosed Messerschmitt 109s
the cold is intense
the cold bites into the body
of each pilot
– Goering he promised
the defence of Southern England
would last exactly four days
and the Royal Air Force four weeks
– *we can for the Führer*
guarantee invasion within a month
but Stuffy Dowding he'd studied
their tactics in Spain
and he pulled us back
wisely from Dunkirk
now in Sir John Soane's
Bentley Priory
his mind moves over maps
– arrows airfields ackack radar
skirmish dogfight battle
if you're alone go home
but he is alone
as he draws out his lines of battle
like an architect
knowing that a battle's somewhere
between algebra
and an architect's drawing
of a crazy changing house
in a hurricane
– house or cathedral where I
and I alone am architect

and my pilots the master masons?
watch how the gothic ornament stands out
in prickly independence
and frosty fortitude
its flying buttresses
and veined foliage
its fearless height of subtle pinnacle
and crested tower
jutting into crockets
or sent like an unperplexed question
up to heaven
– it's both fixed and improvized
this rockety rackety
argument for design
– then I see their brandnew gravestones
like masonic signs
scratched on the base
of this and that pillar
as each manjack of us raises
this unsteady structure
of fabric more divine
than human
or than human praise
as after a trumpet a siren
or a whistle
the shrilled air is stiller
ever so much stiller
then I return to my battle plan
to the fixed the improvized
smashed eggshells and surprise
like an omelette
or soft eggs in isinglass
waiting to be lifted from the crock

– a metal omelette made of swarf
iron filings glycol
and engine oil
– engine oil plus luck
a luck above skill
strategy planning and the
kind of figures that belong
to the more or less exact but boring science
known as quantity surveying
and you need foresight too
that cross in its metal circle
that's a cross
between a moving theorem as it blitzes
across the page
and a shapely a fixed idea
that works if it works
and is beautiful
only in retrospect
like the daystar of Austerlitz
– this is Richard the shit Hillary
who fell out of his Spit-
fire's burning cockpit
into the English Channel
his face and hands badly
– badly and sadly – burnt
for he'd been a handsome young cub
– slightly chubby the face that now needed
a new upper lip
new eyelids
new eyebrows
all chopped and scraped from his legs
the way you pare cheese
or take a spokeshave

to a chair leg
– couldn't know I'd survive
to part the legs
of Merle Oberon
and hug her body like her curvy name
and pit my unburnt cock
against her silky chute
its wet fruit
– my meaty restored body active
my face – buffed under its makeup
my face cubist
stubbed and rubbed
the way you'd stub
your big toe
against a brick wall
as you reached for the sky
– no trace of Buck was ever found
he was a jolly good chap
and a sound pilot
– of the wings on his tunic he said
I reckon these are a oneway ticket pal
'course everyone was determined
to have a squirt at the Hun
we dived into battle our guns
making a tearing sound like hund-
reds of girls ripping sheets of calico

Flight Lieutenant J B Nicholson of 249 Squadron was
flying his Hurricane west of Tangmere at 17,000 feet. He
dived at some Junkers 88s, suddenly his Hurricane
staggered as bullets and cannonballs ripped through the
hood, hit him in the foot and pierced his centre tank. A
searing mass of flame filled the cockpit. He saw the

offender a Me. 110, slide below, and dived hard, the cockpit a furnace, the dashboard dripping like treacle, his hands fused onto the throttle and stuck – *I'll get you you bastard*. He went on firing till the Me. 110 fell out of the sky like a stunned bird, then he struggled out of the cockpit and fell, his mutilated hand feeling for the ripcord. Luckily the rush of air put the flames out, but unluckily the Home Guard shot at him 50 feet above the village of Millbrook in Hampshire. They hit him, but he survived and was awarded the Victoria Cross.

On Battle of Britain Sunday, a primary schoolteacher Miss Eleanor M. Paulin evacuated with her pupils from the East End stands on a leafy road nine miles west of Canterbury, and watches the dogfights in the clear blue sky. Then she sees two Canadian soldiers taking potshots at a German parachutist. Or a parachutist they and she assume is German. Lor, it was shocking, she says later.

the worldwielding shoulders
of a few hundred young pilots
carry the whole burden of this war
don't you ever cry don't ever shed a tear
don't you ever cry after I'm gone
separate and exalted like young gods
who'd closed the gap
between this life this death
a gulf
that was no longer forbidding
– his skin had lifted
it draped his legs like
outsize plusfours
while the skin from his wrists and hands
hung down like paper bags

four spies landed on Romney Marshes
and were sent to the gallows
we were a new race of Englishmen
Peter Pease
one of the old good
the yeoman race
he was killed
as I woke from my dream of his death
then the doctor he tapped lightly
something white that showed
through the granulating knuckle
of my right forefinger
– I'd badly contracting eyelids
keloids
new eyelids and a new
upper lip dead white and thinner
than its predecessor
I felt like a lemon
– a grated lemon or nutmeg
a hearth stone rubbed with hearthstone
but Yorkey Law he'd a completely
new face taken in bacon strips
from his legs
– *you're like meat loaves lads*
said McIndoe
and I saw again those soft white canyons
closed puffballs long pale
embankments cushiony cushnes
flossy nothings hideouts
and then a parachute
like a bulging nappy
it would take months before I'd race the roads
in my battered old Alvis

God how I hate the North
the country the climate the people
all craggy dour and shut in
– north of Oxford I'm in a foreign country
the fighter pilot's emotions
are those of a duellist
– cool precise impersonal
he's privileged to kill well
– from this flight Broody Benson did not return
at night one switched off one's mind
like an electric light
were we really and truly
an harmonious synthesis
of the governing class
and the great rest of England?
– you are well on your way
to becoming a cad
a scabby Jacques
the lad
with a ramshackle face
and a meaty joystick
– Denise her slight figure was in mourning
and she wore no makeup
I put on some brown makeup powder
and asked her
Denise when'll you come out of mourning?
you must lay Peter to rest
Adlertag
their Day of the Eagle
but it was our day
now and ever

A or B in an Anderson Shelter

South London is throughother
like South London
– now in this mother
and father of a raid
we hear each heavy detonation
trying to knock it into shape

Wear White Gloves in the Blackout

To hail a bus or tram
shine a torch on to
your hand

What were they like
            those white gloves in the dark?
– doves or white rabbits
            coming out
        from the conjuror's hat
            or are they his own
            soft gloves laid on
            its black brim?
            or are they Victorian
            suave hidden Edwardian
            play or concertgoers
            who are forever
            trying to hail a cab
            out of the flow and ebb
            of darksome traffic?
            or are they souls by the Styx
            part of death's great wastage?
            or might each hand
            be the thumb and four fingers
            of a Savoy waiter?
        – that's more than enough
        they have to be doves
            that belong not by the dark stream
            but in or on the immense abîme
            that Monsieur Clemenceau dreamed
            then stuffed us in

Violette Szabo

(S.O.E. Ravensbrück)

The love that I have
Of the life that I have
Is yours and yours and yours.
                    Leo Marks

Just when I set a kettle on the stove
   – it's grey a slatecoloured thing
   I hear one of our bombers high above
its fixed clamour its droning
   like chalk scratched
   on a blackboard scratched all along
the empty sky as I light a match
   and the gas whumps in the kitchen of my damp
   call it a cold water flat
with a square window and a lamp
   – it's as though they've already given me a stone
   a stone not bread and I've accepted this cold lump
of granite and climbed it like a mountain
   with a little pack of bread and water
   and my silk poem-code – I do it of my own volition
knowing how in a few years I'll become dead matter
   and will go down into the underworld
   among millions of strange shadows – knowing all that
I love – all those I love – are beyond words
   and that as the kettle starts to sing
   all my young life is like a pint of liquid
hidden inside this small slatecoloured thing
   in yes my now untidy dump
   of a flat where a kettle is about to plump

IN THE BLACKOUT

This poster demands
    a moment's thought
and then it seconds
    that pause that rest
    on the threshold
    the public threshold
    of worn steel
    beyond which
        you might just
    fall or stumble
its two faces
    men's faces – quite impassive –
    one with a soft
    one with a hard hat
    both
    half in light
    like moths
    near an oil lamp
    hard to tell what they feel

Pause as you leave
the station's light

as they watch like detectives
and sieve or seem to sieve
the crowd
like a pair of hourglasses

or they're you and you
your other lives – no
no you're not sure

for at this moment in our lives   we are as leaves
we're blown through its beacon   leaves piled
of electric light   at the station exit
        look at that fool in too much of a hurry
                          and none of us
                          can be sure

they might each be
   ein Detectiv
   waiting for Hans Schleger
or they might be the 8th or the 9th
type of ambiguity

  but before we make the stark

      choice to pause
      before entering the dark
      before we step
      through this door into that dark
      Mr Schleger's poster
      – not *Herr* – *Mister* –
      (and Schleger not Schlegel)
      Mr Schleger's poster
      – but we don't know his name –
      (if we paused again
      we might make out zero)
      we know
      this anonymous poster
      has made the most of
      its own civic poetry
      and will survive
      our pause – yep –
      and our passing

L'Angleterre Tient

Churchill De Gaulle says
peut remuer la lourde pâte anglaise
but why does he keep asking Lloyd George
to join the Cabinet?
he's hardly fresh yeast
– because LG is beginning to look
like England's Pétain – so the Appeasers
may one day soon take charge
– Winston is playing this card
because he wants Hitler to believe
he can still strike a deal
can make us sign a peace
– so LG is the white flag?
– the dummy the pretend white flag
listen if you can get
close enough what you see
is the Union Jack

Klemperer's Diary

In between, we rested a bit at the Dembers, whom we found
alone at table. We talked about politics – cautiously, since the
windows were open.

I kept hold of my balancing pole
and it kept hold of me
I mean my pen like my practical soul
working the lined paper
they made in wartime
– surface rough as a camp hut
and the light on it
on this ruined quire
always murky glauque
the books curtains chairs fixed
by the power that's inside/outside
the power that stacks
the odds against us
so that no matter how steady
my act of witness
I stay anxious as Crusoe
in my improvized study
a prisoner more or less locked
in this shabby hole
who tells himself this must be the fifth act
till I recall that in Hugo's
Cromwell there are six